The Hitchhiker Man

This is the true story of Matt Fox's hitchhiking
adventure to Alaska. Everything you read happened to
Matt starting in the summer of 2007, just after he
graduated from Laurentian university.

Matt Fox

First edition, July 2019

Published in Australia by The Orange Fox Publishing House.

Disclaimer
Some names and identifying characteristics of people, places and
events have been changed to protect the identity of certain
individuals. The story is based on how the author recalls the events
to have happened.

To all those along my journey

Contents

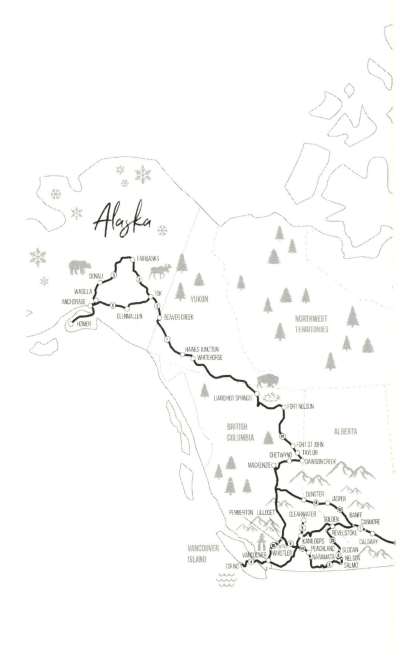

Alaska

FAIRBANKS
DENALI
WASILLA
ANCHORAGE
HOMER
GLENNALLEN
TOK
BEAVER CREEK

YUKON

HAINES JUNCTION
WHITEHORSE

NORTHWEST
TERRITORIES

LIARD HOT SPRINGS
FORT NELSON

BRITISH
COLUMBIA

ALBERTA

FORT ST JOHN
TAYLOR
CHETWYND
DAWSON CREEK
MACKENZIE

DUNSTER
JASPER
GOLDEN
BANFF
CANMORE
REVELSTOKE
CALGARY
PEMBERTON
LILLOOET
CLEARWATER
KAMLOOPS
SLOCAN
PEACHLAND
NELSON
VANCOUVER
ISLAND
WHISTLER
NARAMATA
SALMO
VANCOUVER
TOFINO

THE TIME HAS COME

"Time and effort can get you anything you want in the world. But nothing in the world can get you more time."

The sound of something breathing deeply woke me up from my sleep. The strange noise provided a quick reminder that I was camping in Denali National Park – six million acres of raw Alaskan wilderness. I held my breath and hoped that whatever was beyond the thin fabric wall would go away.

The tent shook violently. I looked around, but I couldn't see in the pitch-black night. Then the tent became still again. I could hear the creature's claws tear the thick Alaskan moss as it circled us. I hoped it wasn't a grizzly, but I had seen so many that morning there was no doubt that it had to be.

My friend Heidi was sleeping peacefully beside me, unaware of the dire situation we were in. I couldn't decide if I should wake her or let her sleep. Then the tent shook again. She had to know. It might be the last time we speak.

I remembered the girl who had given us a ride that morning who had insisted that we got bear spray. She took us to the store to buy some. It was thirty dollars, but I only had fifty to my name, so I left it on the shelf. It seemed like the biggest mistake of my life.

How did I end up in Alaska in the first place? I thought. When only a year before I had been living a normal middle-class life near Toronto. One decision to go hitchhiking had changed the path of my life forever. But I had no regrets for the decisions I had made. I had chosen what I thought was the right path for me and perhaps that path had finally come to its end. I said goodbye to the ones I loved then thanked the universe for the life I had lived before sitting and waiting in silence.

WALKING AWAY
Sudbury, Ontario.

"The more you have, the more you are afraid to lose."

One year earlier in the summer of 2007, I had been living an average Canadian life in Sudbury, a city four hours north of Toronto. I had just graduated from Laurentian university with honours in economics and I was full of potential, drive, and determination. I had even applied for a Master's program in Natural Resource Management. Success seemed like it was waiting just around the corner.

But when a rejection letter arrived in the mail one day, my only plan for the future vanished. I considered getting a job in my field of economics, but the idea of sitting in an office seemed dull and uninviting. I thought about continuing my studies. But what for? I wondered – another office job? More student debt? I had already spent twenty years of my life in school.

With no pressure on me to follow a certain path I spent my time enjoying the warm days of the summer while avoiding any real-life decisions. That is until one night when an unexpected plan for my future arrived. It was late into a night of drinking with my friend Ryan when he first mentioned his intention to hitchhike across Canada. I wondered how he could have devised such a foolish and risky plan. I didn't know a single person who had hitchhiked before and I realised that my knowledge of it was limited to what I had seen on the news. I had never picked up a hitchhiker either, as I thought the risks were too great.

The next morning I woke up with a splitting headache and a blurred memory of the night before. For some reason I felt uneasy about something. I thought long and hard until I realised that I had agreed to go hitchhiking across Canada with Ryan.

Thankfully I also remembered that the person Ryan had originally planned to go on the trip with had just bailed, so I knew it wouldn't be a big deal when I told him that I wasn't going to go either. When I finally crawled out of bed, my life seemed to be fully in order again.

With each day that passed I thought of telling Ryan that I wasn't going to go on the trip with him. But each time I was about to visit or call with my decision I was forced to consider my alternatives. I had always wondered what the rest of Canada looked like, so naturally I wondered about where Ryan would go and what he would see.

I had always thought that travelling was expensive, but for the first time in my life it seemed as if it was within my grasp. I stared at the walls of my room covered in pictures of beautiful and exciting places – beaches, mountains, the tropics, and rain forests. All the places I dreamed of visiting one day and part of the reason I worked so hard in university.

The more I tried to talk myself out of the trip, the more reasons I found to go. Hitchhiking seemed like a way to make my dreams of travelling come true. With plenty of common sense, perhaps it could even be safe. I asked my friends what they thought of the adventure, but to my dismay they all thought it was a terrible idea. And I could understand why since I thought the same thing they did. It made me wonder how anybody could have a valid opinion on something they had never experienced. But I knew that I was no different from them, since I also spent my life formulating my own inexperienced opinions. It seemed as if the only way to know what would happen on the road was to travel that road. After contemplating it for some time I finally decided I was going to take the chance.

LEAVING EVERYTHING FOR NOTHING
Sudbury Ontario. 0 km.

"The difference between insanity and genius is measured only by success."
—Masashi Kishimoto

To prepare for the journey that lay ahead I donated most of my stuff to the local thrift shop. Deep down inside I was aware that the memories my simple possessions triggered would be gone forever. After two weeks of clearing my stuff out I was left with only what I could fit into my backpack.

The evening before my departure my friends came over to say goodbye and the mood was sombre. We talked about where the road might take me and the misadventures that could happen along the way. A few even tried to talk me out of it, but my mind was already made up. I promised that one day I would return.

I went to bed in my empty room and nostalgia took over

my thoughts. I felt alone in there, aware that only a few days earlier it had been the most comfortable place in my world. Now the space was almost entirely empty and my only possessions were my backpack and guitar. I couldn't sleep. Instead my mind raced with all the scenarios I would inevitably face on the road. Could Ryan and I actually get all the way across Canada? Would we be safe? Was this actually a really bad idea? It was hard to imagine finding happiness on the road. A life with no home seemed almost unfathomable.

On the morning of our departure I got out of bed, scared of what lay ahead. The cool morning air was ominous and uninviting. I couldn't explain even to myself why I was going that day.

CHANGE COMES FAST
Sudbury, Ontario. 0 km.

"Those who speak don't know, and those who know don't speak."
—Lao Tzu

I packed my toothbrush into my bag before zipping it back up one last time. I said goodbye to my sister who I had been living with. She was sad to see me go, but made no attempt to stop me. Neither one of us knew if I would return.

It was six in the morning when I walked down the steps of my townhouse on my way to Ryan's place. He was already outside waiting for me when I got there. We crossed the street and walked through the mall with all our possessions on our backs. I think it was the most depressing moment of my life, but there was no turning back. I had told too many people I was going to go. Staying seemed like a failure. An inability to carry through with what I had said I was going to do. I wondered if my ego had gotten the best of me.

Ryan and I took the city bus to the outskirts of the Sudbury, the place I had spent the last five years living while studying. At the last stop the driver pulled over and looked back at us. It was my last chance to bail on the trip and the thought was very much on my mind. I could simply take the bus back to my place, have a hot shower, and get back into my comfy bed like nothing had ever happened. It was the perfect plan, but for some reason I picked up my bag and I walked off the bus.

The weight of my backpack became obvious almost immediately. The short walk to the Trans-Canada Highway seemed like a trek through the Himalayas. When we finally arrived at the edge of the highway, my shoulders ached. But we smiled and put our thumbs out, excited to begin our journey.

Countless cars drove by while the morning sun rose into the clear blue sky. I felt optimistic, but as each hour passed my optimism began to fade. The pavement absorbed the sun's heat and radiated it back up at us. By the time it was at its peak we were both drenched in sweat. I looked back at the city shimmering in the heat haze, the place where we had come from just six hours earlier. Even if we didn't get a ride, I decided that I wasn't going back there. I didn't want to walk through the same door in my life that I had just closed.

At first I felt as if the people driving by were my fellow motorists, my fellow humans. The ones that I shared the road with daily. Yet after hours of watching cars pass by the connection seemed to disappear. Instead I could feel the motorists' piercing eyes judging us, categorising us, and then forgetting us. As if we were trying to get something that we didn't deserve.

What if they knew that I still had a car sitting in my driveway at home? Would that make a difference? Would they give me a ride if they knew I was a contributing member of society? None of that seemed to matter anymore. In less than one day I had become just another blank face to forget. It was hard to take it all in. In such a short amount of time I had become an outcast, a rebel, and a vagabond.

Ryan and I walked endlessly, desperate to cover some distance by foot seeing as the passing cars weren't helping. The straps of my bag were cutting into my shoulders. One arm ached from holding my twelve-string guitar while the other hurt from holding out my thumb. After ten hours of hitching and no rides we dropped our bags on the ground, demoralised. But right then at the lowest point of our day a shiny red Ford truck pulled over. A young guy named Mike offered to take us a few km up the road.

As if the gates to a forbidden kingdom had just been unlocked, the doors of the hitchhiking world swung open in front of us. Then Mike kindly set us down in front of a burger joint some ten minutes later, where we celebrated our first ride with some food and tried to forget about the painful day behind us.

We had not travelled far, but in the short amount of time on the road my view of the world had already begun to change. For the first time in my life I understood how quickly somebody who escaped the claws of society could become alienated forever.

We walked back to the road with a new-found optimism, but again no cars stopped and again we gave up on walking.

Instead we sat down on the warm pavement. I played guitar and worked on some songs, and we took turns putting our thumbs out.

At some point a blue GMC truck screeched to a stop in front of us.

"Where you boys headed?" an old man wearing a cowboy hat asked.

"Across Canada," we replied.

"Well, I'm only going to the next town, but it'll be further than where yer sittin' now."

We climbed into the truck. The guy driving was named Frank and he looked like a farmer. After a few pleasantries he dropped us off in the little town of Massey, Ontario, on the edge of Georgian Bay. As the last few rays of sun left the sky, we cracked a beer to celebrate our semi-successful first day of hitchhiking. We packed up and were about to head into the bushes for the night when a white Mazda four-door pulled over beside us.

THE JOURNEY BEGINS
Massey, Ontario. 112 km.

"Only those who will risk going too far can possibly find out how far it is possible to go."
—T.S. Elliot

We weren't quite sure if the Mazda had stopped for us or for some other reason. The car had Quebec plates, but nobody emerged and no window went down. We took another uncertain step towards the forest when the driver's door flew open. A man with a French accent introduced himself as Pierre, then helped us put our bags in the trunk. We sat down on the comfortable leather seats, Pierre put on some French rap music, and then we drove off into the darkness.

He seemed pleased to have some company. "I've been driving for twelve hours straight," he told us in his strong French accent. Travelling through the night at a hundred km an hour with a stranger who was at the limits of exhaustion didn't seem like the best idea. But at that moment Pierre falling asleep at the wheel seemed to be the greatest of all my worries, which in a sense was reassuring.

Pierre's English was limited, but the conversation flowed nonetheless. He was on his way to Alberta to help his brother because his restaurant was understaffed. After a few hours, Ryan said, "Hey, if you get tired, I have family not too far from here, they live on the highway and we're all welcome to stay the night."

"I will think about it," Pierre replied. After a few more hours of driving, Pierre accepted the offer on the condition that we were back on the road at six the next morning. It was past midnight when we pulled into the sleepy little town of Wawa, Ontario, on the edge of Lake Superior. Ryan's girlfriend's parents' house was just off the highway and after some food and a few beers we all went to bed exhausted.

Despite being tired I couldn't sleep that night, and instead I reflected on all that I had experienced that day. I had travelled over five hundred km, which was surprising. It was the farthest distance I had ever travelled in a single day. I thought of my friends back in Sudbury, living life like nothing had changed. Yet my life was upside down now and I had a strange suspicion that it would never be the same again.

DIRTY AND GREY
Winnipeg, Manitoba. 1686 km.

"Not all those who wander are lost."
—J.R.R. Tolkien

We were on the road first thing in the morning and I was happy to be in the backseat. I shut my eyes the moment we drove off and awoke to the view of beautiful rolling hills lined with evergreen trees. The road hugged the coast of the great Lake Superior.

I had been so worried about all the bad things that I thought might happen on the trip that I forgot that I might actually have a good time. Yet there I was enjoying spectacular views of places I had never seen before. The company was entertaining and venturing into the unknown was exciting.

Pierre was on a mission to get to Alberta as quickly as possible, so the only stops we made were to fill up the gas tank. After ten hours on the road we crossed the border into Manitoba and shortly after we started to see signs for

Winnipeg. Our destination was the ocean in British Columbia and the thought of getting to Alberta as quickly as we were was a dream come true. At the rate we were going, we could make it to the ocean in less than a week. But Ryan had other plans.

"Hey man," Ryan said while looking back at me, "one of my friends lives in Winnipeg. Do you want to stop there for a few days?" He caught me off guard. I was so focussed on our destination that I hadn't considered taking an excursion. But I was open to anything.

"Sure man," I replied.

"Sweet," Ryan said.

I was a bit disappointed that we were going to give up a ride that could take us so far. When I saw the grey smog hovering over the city of Winnipeg, I was sure that I didn't want to get out of the car. But I kept my thoughts to myself. As we approached the city, we saw two guys that looked like seasoned hitchhikers walking along the sidewalk carrying big backpacks.

"Pierre, can you drop us off here please?"

"Oui, oui," he said with a smile before pulling up to the curb.

We thanked him and jumped out. Then we briskly crossed the street and trotted until we caught up with the other backpackers. They looked dirty, but with nothing to lose we approached them and introduced ourselves.

"Hey, how's it going?" I asked from behind to grab their attention.

"Good, you?" They both replied at the same time with a

smile. They were both filthy, stank, and looked like they hadn't washed in a while.

"Are you guys hitchhiking?" I asked, getting straight to the point.

"Yeah man, are you?"

"Yup, it's our first time. We just hitchhiked from Sudbury."

"Oh man! Did you guys get stuck in Wawa?"

"No, we had a ride stay the night with us at his girlfriend's parents house," I replied.

"Oh man, you guys are lucky! We always get stuck in Wawa, sometimes for days. It's impossible to get a ride out of that place."

"I guess we got lucky to get one all the way through then, eh?" Ryan replied.

"What are your plans for the night?" I asked, aware that the sun was already setting and anxious to find a spot to sleep before it got dark. "We know of a good place to camp a few blocks from here. We were just going to grab some food and then go set up. You guys want to join us?"

We gladly agreed, happy to have a safe spot to sleep in the city. We walked with them to a store to get some food.

Along the way we found out that their names were Sam and Mike and that they were both from Calgary. But they had been hitchhiking back and forth across Canada for years. Their filth was not a good representation of their character as they both seemed like good people.

Mike ran into the shop and left his bag with Sam.

"Hey Sam, can you watch my bag too?" I asked

He scolded me instead.

"Hey man, you don't know me so don't trust me with all your belongings. I did the same thing when I first started hitchhiking, except the dude said he would watch my stuff and when I got out of the store it was all gone. I was left with nothing. It sucked. Just keep your stuff in sight if you don't want to lose it. Some people are desperate on the streets, man."

"Thanks for the advice, makes sense."

It was a good lesson to learn. It also re-assured me that Sam and Mike were honest people, even though it looked like they didn't have a dollar to their names.

When we finished shopping, we followed Sam and Mike along a busy road towards a large bridge that appeared to go into the city. The last rays of the sun left the sky just as we arrived at the bridge. Instead of crossing it, we turned right down a little dirt track and headed straight into Winnipeg's Central Park. A place that is notorious for being extremely dangerous at night. I wondered what we had got ourselves into. Sam said, "I wouldn't wander around the park at night, it's not safe. But we know of a secret spot where we've never had any trouble."

We walked through the darkness and I seriously questioned if what we were doing was a good idea, but I didn't say a word. I was exhausted from sitting in the car all day and just wanted to sit down, relax, and then go to bed.

We arrived at a clearing that was surrounded by piles of yard waste and grass clippings on one side and a chain-link fence on the other. I could see the buildings of the city all lit up in the distance. The streets were full of cars racing out of town, surely all going to have dinner in their comfortable homes. Just like I would have only a few days before. Instead of a nice comfy bed and dinner at a table, my life choices had sent me to a dangerous park to sleep for the night. I remembered the twelve-inch machete I had brought in my bag for protection from bears. I wondered if perhaps it wasn't a wild animal that I would need it for.

"Well, this is home for the night," Sam said. We dropped our bags on the ground. I took a quick walk to survey our surroundings. I wanted to know exactly what was around us. I stood in the shadows and I could see a path that led deeper into the park. There were figures on benches and on the grass, but they didn't notice me in the shadows. Satisfied, I crept back to our campsite. Ryan and I set up our tent while Sam and Mike built a fire. I hadn't imagined having a fire in Winnipeg Central Park. In fact, I had been hoping to draw as little attention as possible to our location. But the night had become a bit chilly and the warmth of the fire was nice.

"Aren't you guys going to put up tents?" I asked Sam and Mike.

"Nah, we just sleep in our sleeping bags under the stars," they replied.

Mike pulled out a tiny speaker and put on some music while our cans of chilli heated up in the campfire. Everything was shaping up nicely – we had made friends and we had music, accommodation, warmth, beers, and the Winnipeg skyline in the distance. Besides being in the most dangerous park in Canada, things weren't too bad.

"So where have you guys hitchhiked? I asked.

"Just across Canada, but from coast to coast three times already."

"That's a lot of hitching" I replied while swatting at a swarm of mosquitos. I wondered how the guys could possibly sleep comfortably with all the bugs.

"Yeah, we've been on the road for years. We kind of just left and never looked back. Some days are hard, but it beats working for the Man."

"Yeah, I guess."

"There is a lot you learn on the road when you don't have money. How to survive with nothing. Dumpster diving for food, going to shelters. Man, grocery stores dumpsters are full of good food to eat. They fill them up every night with old food."

I had never heard of dumpster diving before, but I guess when you're hungry and have no money you have to find food somewhere.

"So how was your trip here?" Sam asked, changing the subject.

"Well, we struggled to get a ride all day yesterday, we must have walked ten kilometres," Ryan said.

"Walked?" Sam replied with a look of confusion on his face. "Don't walk, that's a rookie mistake. When you walk everybody thinks you're going to get there eventually and nobody stops. If you just sit and wait on the side of the road people know the only way you are going to get anywhere is with a ride."

It made sense, I thought. We didn't get any rides when

we were walking. We chatted until we finished our beers. Then, tired of fending off the mosquitos, we all went to bed.

I didn't bring a tent on the trip because Ryan had told me that I could share his two-man. I just hadn't realized that a two-man tent literally only fits two people with no extra space for our stuff. Worried about our bags getting stolen while we slept, we tied them to our feet and put them just outside the tent door. We put my guitar in between us in the tent and I put my machete close by my side. Nobody could run off with our bags without waking us up, and surely I had a bigger knife than any thief would have.

I faced many of my fears that night. I was further from my comfort zone than I had ever been before. I had abandoned my cosy bed back at home for a dangerous park with no glamour. What had I been thinking? Halfway through the night trains started passing by on the tracks some twenty feet from our tent. The ground rumbled while the trains clanged away.

I felt more alone than I had ever felt before. I wondered what I was really expecting out of our adventure. How could I have possibly thought that hitchhiking was a good idea? But the realization was arriving a few days too late.

When the trains finally stopped in the early morning, I was finally able to fall asleep for a short period of time before the sun's heat made the tent unbearable to be inside. When I finally looked out, our friends were already gone. Again, we were alone so we packed up the campsite and made our way into the city.

We spent the day exploring the sights while trying to get

a hold of Ryan's friend on a pay phone. Late in the afternoon we started looking for hostels to stay in to avoid another night in the park, but they were all too expensive.

Just as the evening was approaching, Ryan tried one last time to get a hold of his friend Pat, and at last was successful. Pat drove into the city and picked us up. Then he thankfully took us out of the city to his house in the suburbs. When I walked through the door, I realised from the decorating that Pat still lived with his parents, but it was way better than being in the park downtown.

We had dinner with Pat's family. The ornaments and trinkets that decorated the living room reminded me of all that I had left behind. At dinner, Pat said, "So I'm going to a three-day music festival called the Winnipeg Folk Fest this weekend. Do you guys want to come too?" With very little money, buying tickets was not an option. But by the time we went to bed, we had devised a plan to sneak into the festival.

The next day we gathered all the necessary supplies for three days of partying. Then we looked over maps of the festival grounds, examined the fence lines and tried to predict where the security guards would be. By the time we went to bed, the van was packed and we had hatched a plan to sneak in. It was starting to feel like nothing was going to be easy on our trip.

THE WINNIPEG
FOLK FESTIVAL
Winnipeg, Manitoba. 1686 km.

"If you satisfy a desire, you will desire more. If you desire nothing, it is easy to be content."

In the morning we drove half an hour to Birds Hill Provincial Park, which was twenty-five kilometres north of Winnipeg. I was nervous when we arrived at the gates. The roads were full of people and cars and there was an electric energy in the air. It was my first time sneaking into a festival and I felt the odds were stacked against me.

As we drove through the first checkpoint my heart raced. But the lady at the booth didn't ask us for tickets, instead she just told us where to go. We continued along the road into the National Park until we saw the entrance to the campground, our destination. Pat drove past the entrance and then stopped on the side of the road.

"This is it guys," he said. "Go quickly and I'll see you inside."

Ryan and I jumped out of the van, leaving all our belongings behind. It was our plan of course. But it hadn't occurred to me until then that if I got caught and escorted from the festival, I had no way of getting my stuff or contacting the guys. I would be stuck with no money, no tent, and nothing to my name in the middle of nowhere. I should have at least got Pat's phone number but it was already too late. The van was gone.

Two security guards walked by while we stood awkwardly on the side of the road, but they took no notice of us. When they had gone, we followed the path they had been using, and walked halfway around the perimeter of the campground until we were alone. Then we trekked into the bushes and arrived at a barbed wire fence. Surprisingly it was the only thing separating us from the tents on the other side. We carefully climbed over the fence, then swiftly zigzagged through the trees. I looked back periodically to make sure we weren't being followed by security, but they were nowhere to be seen.

The hard part was done. We just had to find Pat and our mission would be a success. The campground was full of people setting up colourful tents and tepees while others hung sarongs, banners, and flags. Peoples' marquees were filled with couches, tables, stoves, and rugs. All the luxuries of home.

The electric vibe in the campground melted away most of the doubts I had about our journey. The transition had been extreme, going from sleeping in the scariest place I had ever slept one night into a seemingly peaceful paradise the next. After a little searching we found Pat sitting with a circle of his friends drinking beer. As we approached, they cheered and threw us drinks. Most of my worries seemed to vanish, aware that my belongings were once again by my side.

After spending the day in the sun with Pat's friends, Ryan and I decided to go and find some mushrooms for the evening. We grabbed a few beers and wandered through the campground. Although we were searching for mushrooms, almost everybody we asked invited us to join them for a drink at their campsite. After each, we left new friends behind.

I was overwhelmed with how friendly everybody was. Every person made us feel like we were back at home with the best of friends. The old saying goes 'that home is where the heart is,' and for the first time in my life I was starting to understand what it meant.

After hours of wandering we were finally pointed in the direction of a mythical tepee, which after some tedious searching we were able to locate. A short while later we walked away with seven grams of small red mushrooms, nothing like any I had ever seen before. The dealer's words echoed through my head: "No matter what you do, do not eat more than a gram of those at a time."

When we arrived back at the campsite, it was already empty. The guys had gone to listen to music. But since we didn't have wristbands, we were stuck in the campground until we decided to sneak into the music venue across the road. But we were in no rush to go anywhere. Instead, Ryan and I just sat back, rolled up a joint, and enjoyed another beer.

LOOKING DEEPER WITHIN
Winnipeg Folk Festival. 1686 km.

"At the centre of your being, you have the answer; you know who you are and you know what you want."
—Lao Tzu

We measured out what looked like a gram of mushrooms each. I stuffed the putrid things down my throat and followed them with chocolate. I had never enjoyed the taste of mushrooms and I was happy once my taste buds were free of their earthy spores.

We packed a bag with beers and went to wander the campground some more. It wasn't long before I felt the first wave of mushrooms roll in. As always, the trip started with a strangely uncomfortable feeling, close to one of nausea. For a while I felt as if I was trapped within my own body, desperate to get out. Wave after wave shuddered through my body, and each was a little bit more powerful than the one before.

The initial feeling of nausea was replaced by a euphoric

body high. It felt as if energy was flowing freely out of me in every direction. At that moment I became aware of a drum beat thumping in the distance. My body insisted that it be taken to the sound and my mind accepted the request without questioning it. As if all at once my mind became only a mere observer of all that was going on around me, instead of the controller of my being.

Time seemed to slow down. My brain processed my surroundings with a heightened sense of awareness. I felt as if my consciousness had expanded. I became acutely aware of the thousands of interactions that were taking place between my body and its surroundings at every moment. The same interactions that were normally filtered out by my brain for reasons I could not explain.

Ryan and I progressed slowly towards the sound of the drums. The speed with which we travelled towards our destination seemed to decrease almost exponentially. As my awareness grew, I felt as if I had become a mere spectator in all that was happening around me.

My body seemed to be operating of its own accord and the tribal beats were its sole focus. I was not concerned that our pace had slowed to almost a crawl. The sound of the drums seemed to resonate within every cell in my body, subconsciously pulling me closer to their source. I felt as if I had gone back in time, to where my ancestors lived a simple life and danced to the beat of the drums around the fire. To my time in the womb where the sole sound I heard was the beating of my mother's heart. Who I was and where I was seemed insignificant.

At last we left the tents of the campground behind. Before us there was an open plane, packed with people dancing. I almost couldn't believe my eyes. Thousands of people danced in costumes, others spun fire nearby. I felt as if we had just trekked through a thick jungle and had finally reached its edge. Then the thumping tribal beats took control of my body and pulled me in.

Like a bug drawn to light, I moved towards the sound, dancing, shaking, and smiling my way through the crowds of people. At last I could see that the source of the music was a drum circle on top of the nearby hill. Slowly, I ascended it, until at last I arrived at the top. Fifty drums were all being played there, generating an energy that I had never before experienced.

I danced around the drummers mesmerised. At some point I was offered a place within the circle that I gladly accepted. I found myself rhythmically thumping on a djembe in unison with the others. For the first time that I could remember I felt as if I was finally reconnecting with who I was.

My comprehension of life seemed to grow. So many of the questions I had about life seemed to answer themselves as the mushrooms expanded my neural pathways and forged new connections. Thoughts that fuelled my ego and which I had believed in my entire life became meaningless, and I felt as if my journey had finally begun.

I joined the dance floor again. This time a girl danced towards me. Each time I looked up our eyes met. We moved closer to each other, our hands touching and our bodies joined together as one. She moved her hands up and down my body, then grabbed my hand and pulled me somewhere quiet. We enjoyed the warmth of each other's bodies in the cool night air.

Many questions I had tried to solve for years got answered that night. I walked back through the campground in the bright morning sunlight, happy that I had taken the chance and gone hitchhiking. When I finally arrived at the tent, I found Ryan already fast asleep. I put my head down on my pillow and listened to the drums still thumping in the distance, totally content.

MORE MUSHROOMS
Winnipeg Folk Festival. 1686 km.

"Everything you've ever wanted is on the other side of fear."
—George Adair

I woke up late with no doubts left in my mind that I had made the right decision to go hitchhiking. I could not have imagined in my wildest dreams that I would have had one of the best nights of my life only a few days into the journey.

It didn't take long before Ryan and I had agreed to eat more of the mushrooms. But this time we decided to split the rest of the bag in half and eat two and a half grams each. I ignored the words of the dealer that echoed in my head: "do not eat more than a gram of those at a time." But that was just for the first night I imagined. I had heard of a rule for eating mushrooms that recommends that you eat twice as many on the second consecutive day of tripping if you want to get the same high as the first day. It sounded reasonable.

Just before the sun set we ate the mushrooms, then sat in the forest waiting for our trips to begin. It didn't take long before I began to experience wild hallucinations, the trees warped and twisted. The branches moved closer and then further away from me as if they were alive and breathing. My body overflowed with euphoria.

With each breath I took I seemed to develop a deeper connection with all that was around me. As if we were all just one big living and breathing organism. I wondered if perhaps everything I could see was just one big dream. Everything justified because of my ability to see it all through my eyes. But perhaps my eyes were the illusion. An illusion created by my mind to justify all that I perceived.

The mushrooms took full control of me – unable to move my body, all I could do was hold on for the ride. I felt like a deadweight stuck on the bottom of the ocean. I looked at Ryan sitting beside me and I knew that he was in deep as well. I was desperate for a pee but no matter how much I willed myself to get out of the chair, I was unable to control the movement of my body.

The daylight faded and darkness set in. I felt as if I was a prisoner trapped in a jail that I had created for myself. Hours passed before I finally regained some control of my mind. When at last I was finally able to control my body, I used all my power and effort to get up out of the chair. But to my horror, as I stood up my legs failed and I fell to the ground. Desperate to not get stuck for another indefinite amount of time, I called upon the powers of the gods and used all my might to jump back up to my feet as quickly as I could. I stumbled over to a tree and prepared to release my bladder. I thought that maybe after I took a pee, I would go and dance.

I unzipped my jeans and it felt as if the gates to a dam had been opened. Just as the pee began to flow, I felt a strange rumbling coming from my stomach. I could feel something rushing from within towards my throat and I leaned forward to aim the puke away from myself. But just as the puke hit my throat, I lost control of my arms and my legs while still conscious. I watched in horror as I fell face first into the pine tree I was peeing against. I hit hard and could hear the branches snap as I slid down the trunk to the ground. Then there was darkness.

"Matt, Matt! Hey, Matt!" The sound echoed in my head but I couldn't quite pinpoint it or understand where it was coming from. Who was Matt I wondered? "Matt, Matt," the voice echoed again. The name seemed very familiar, I was sure I knew someone called Matt, but who could he be I wondered. I was sure he was someone close to me. Then it clicked. I was Matt. I was hitchhiking. I was at a festival, I did mushrooms, my memories flooded back all at once. I was peeing, then I passed out. I opened my eyes and could feel pine needles in my mouth. I tried to roll over but my hand was stuck under me, still holding my penis. I dragged my hand out then I pushed myself up off the ground, and I pulled up my pants. Ryan was standing there and he looked concerned. "Are you all right man?" he asked. "Uh, yeah, I'm fine," I replied unconvincingly.

A second later I started projectile vomiting again. Stream after stream flowed from my mouth until there was nothing left. The convulsions continued, I dry heaved over and over as my body desperately tried to expel the poison. At some point I stumbled to the tent and crawled inside. My head was pounding with a splitting headache, the thought of dancing had left my mind as I was in no state to go anywhere. I spent the rest of the night lying in my sleeping bag with my eyes open, listening to the drum circle in the distance. When the sun rose in the morning, I was finally able to fall asleep.

On the last day of the festival we were given some wristbands to go watch the music. But I still felt sick from the night before and only saw a bit before going back to my tent for an early sleep. The next morning when we were having breakfast, a guy named Mike walked up to the campsite and asked if anybody needed a ride west. It was the perfect chance for us to continue our journey, but we had already planned to stay at Pat's for a night before we left Winnipeg.

The festival had been a monumental success. I was happy we had taken the gamble. That night we had dinner at Pat's house. We reminisced about the great time we had at the festival. I went to bed with a smile on my face while still feeling a bit nervous about the long road ahead.

THE WEST IS BEST
Winnipeg, Manitoba. 1686 km.

"Change is the only constant in life."
—Heraclitus

The next morning Pat dropped us off at a truck stop on the Trans-Canada Highway just west of Winnipeg. We threw our bags onto the side of the road and then waved to Pat as he drove off. Surprisingly, I was happy to be on the highway again. But I was sad to be leaving another place where I had felt comfortable. Even though it had only been a week since I left home, I was no longer as scared of the unknown.

We stood at the edge of the Canadian Prairies, a place I had always dreamed of visiting. Endless fields of grassland went as far as the eye could see without a single tree in sight. We waited in the same spot for hours, but it no longer felt like a chore. It was actually kind of nice being alone in the wilderness, watching life go by. Especially since we decided to never walk with our bags again.

Ryan went into the gas station to grab a snack while I

kept hitchhiking. A moment after he had walked off, a grey Jeep pulled over. I walked up to the window to see where it was going, but when I got there I saw Mike – the guy that had offered us a ride west at the festival.

"Throw your bags in the back and hop in," he said enthusiastically.

"Oh, actually my friend is in the store grabbing some stuff, are you happy to take both of us?"

The look on his face changed dramatically as he looked into the back of his jeep. The rear seat was packed almost to the roof with bags that looked like they had been thrown in there by a drunk person in a hurry.

"Sorry, I just don't think I have room for two people," he said with a hint of disappointment.

Then he jumped out of the jeep and started examining the pile of luggage from another angle with the same confused look on his face. The logical thing to do would have been to put up the back seat and to organise the luggage. However, after a little contemplation Mike said, "actually, I think one of you can just sit on the luggage if you want."

I was flabbergasted by his decision-making process, but I was in no position to question him. When Ryan came back from the store, we stuffed our luggage into the chaotic mess in the back. Ryan crawled in on top of the bags and I jumped into the front with Mike. We were back on the road and heading west.

Once the Jeep was up to speed Mike looked over at me and said, "do you puff?"

"Oh yeah," I replied with a smile.

"Sweet!"

He threw an ounce on my lap, "all right, you roll and I'll drive."

"Sounds good to me!"

Mike was a nurse from Toronto who had just taken a six-month leave from work to travel across Canada. Like us he had never been across the country before and was excited to see British Colombia.

The road was as straight as a ruler and the landscape was as flat as a pancake. It was exactly how I had imagined the prairies to be. We drove by some salt flats, but they were the most exciting thing to see, the rest of the highway was lined with fields. Mike was not the best driver, he swerved regularly and seemed to have trouble driving down the straight road. On top of that, he kept asking me how his driving was. I didn't want to be rude, so time and time again I told him it was fine.

Finally, he turned and looked me in the eyes before he said, "Honestly, is my driving okay?"

"To be totally honest with you," I replied as kindly as possible, "you have been swerving quite a bit."

"Shit," he said, followed by, "can you drive? I'm still tripping on acid from the festival."

I jumped behind the wheel and drove off. Not long after both the guys fell asleep. The landscape was bare, and besides the grass fields there was nothing to see in any direction. Eventually Mike woke up and decided to go sleep on the stack of luggage in the back. Ryan hopped in the front with me and I couldn't help but laugh as I looked at him sitting in the passenger seat beside me. Somehow, we were in full control of a brand-new Jeep.

Ryan and I took turns driving through the night. When we needed gas, we would wake Mike up and he would run inside, pay, and then go right back to sleep on top of the luggage. Finally, when daylight arrived Mike decided to hop in the front again and I was happy to take my turn sleeping on the bags. It was as uncomfortable as I had imagined, but I eventually managed to fall asleep.

We drove through Saskatchewan that night and early in the morning we saw signs for Calgary. I had a good friend named Danny who lived there and I was hoping to meet up with him for a night. Mike had been hoping that we would drive across the rest of Canada with him and seemed a bit disappointed when he mentioned to him that we would be parting ways in Calgary. My perspective had changed from just a week before. Instead of wanting to rush across Canada, I was a lot more interested in taking my time and enjoying the journey.

Mike dropped us off in downtown Calgary on a street full of people wearing cowboy hats, tight jeans, and leather boots. It seemed like we were in another country. We had travelled around 3000 km, further than I had ever travelled by car before. I was surprised to say the least. I had spent my whole life in the same place. If I had of known that I could travel to the other side of the country so easily, I think I would have done it years ago. But I reassured myself that there was no point in thinking about things that I could have done differently. Instead I focused my thoughts on what I could do to make my life better in the future.

COWBOYS AND MOUNTAINS
Calgary, Alberta. 3024 km.

"Better to see something once, than to hear about it a thousand times."
—Ancient proverb

I used a pay phone to call my friend Danny and he came to meet us in a beige Infiniti G45 coupe, a fancy little sports car that seemed to have every feature you could imagine except room for luggage. After half an hour of rearranging our bags we were miraculously able to fit into the car.

"Does everybody normally dress in cowboy boots around here?" I asked Danny.

"Ha ha. No, everyone's just dressed up for the Calgary Stampede."

We drove through downtown and every bar was packed. Since we didn't have much money to spend Danny suggested taking us into the mountains. So we headed north and left the city behind. We drove past the ski jumps from the 1988 Calgary Winter Olympics. I could see the Rocky

Mountains on the horizon and I started to get butterflies in my stomach. My whole life I had dreamt of seeing them and for the first time they were actually within my view.

The flat landscape was soon replaced by vertical rocks towering into the heavens, with evergreen trees climbing their sides. The massive peaks asserted their dominance over everything within their domain. Each mountain peak was unique and magnificent in its own way and the deeper we drove into the mountains, the more breathtaking they became.

My entire existence had been spent living in cities covered with cement with little of the Earth's natural terrain visible. As we drove into the mountains, I realised that for the first time in my life I was in a place where nature overpowered humans. I was finally able to see nature flourish in its original form. The giant peaks made me feel insignificant and humble. They were the most beautiful thing I had ever seen.

It was dark when we arrived in the resort town of Banff. Danny found a hostel for him and his girlfriend while Ryan and I set up our tent in the bushes. It was our first time camping in bear territory and there were piles of droppings near where we pitched the tent. I crawled inside and fell asleep to the sound of the river rapids somewhere below us.

In the morning Danny gave us a grand tour of the area. We saw mountain goats, caribou, and a beautiful turquoise lake. The size of the animals we saw was alarming and I was quite aware that we had just shuffled a few steps lower on the food chain.

LIFE IS ABOUT THE MOMENT
Golden, B.C. 3306 km.

"The journey, not the destination matters…"
—T.S. Elliot

Danny dropped us off at the entrance to the highway, then headed back to Calgary. Ryan and I walked along the on ramp and sat down at a good spot to hitchhike. I played my guitar while staring at the snow-capped mountains in the distance. Wild roses lined the side of the highway, and I knew we had a long road ahead.

A guy named Pete pulled over in a big SUV and within moments of driving off with him, he told us that he was going to B.C. to grab a few pounds of high-quality weed. "It's way cheaper in B.C.," he explained, "so I do the trip every once and a while."

It amazed me how quickly people told us their secrets when we were hitchhiking. I figured it was because they never expected to see us again.

The winding highway began to follow the curves of the

mountains. Large inclines were followed by massive descents. It was a refreshing change from the flat, straight road we had driven through the prairies.

"I have a cousin that lives in Golden B.C.," Ryan mentioned. It was the next town on the map. "Did you want to stop there and try to meet up with her?" he added.

It was another unexpected interruption to our journey and I wondered why Ryan waited until the last moment to mention his plans to me. But there was no point in over-thinking things. "Sounds good to me," I replied. When we arrived in Golden, Pete dropped us off at a gas station and we parted company.

Golden, B.C. is a small ski town in a big valley. There were only a few shops and a single restaurant on the main street. In the distance I could see the ski runs climbing the slope of the mountain. Ryan's cousin Samantha and her boyfriend Paul picked us up in a four by four Tracker. They took us on a twenty-minute drive south to their little cabin, which was right on the Columbia River. They cooked us a fresh fish dinner, then we had a campfire and drank some beers. As the fire warmed us we listened to Paul tell us stories about bears he had seen in the woods nearby.

The next day Paul took us up the river in his boat. We stopped at a dock that was floating in the middle of the river. We drank a few beers and then swam in the murky brown water. Most of the trees on the river bank were almost totally submerged in the river as a result of the yearly snow melt. Although the brown soupy water was not inviting, it was the only way to escape the hundreds of black flies that were feasting on us.

"I'm heading west later this week if you boys want to catch a ride with me. As long as you don't mind hanging around until I leave," Paul said. The offer of a ride with someone familiar sounded great to both of us, so we accepted.

A few days later we loaded the Tracker with all our gear. The starter didn't work, so one of us would have to climb under the truck and bang the starter with a hammer while someone else cranked the ignition each time we wanted to start it up.

It was seven in the morning when we pulled out of the driveway. Golden had started to feel like home, but it was just another place we were leaving behind. We drove west on the highway for a few hours before Paul pulled the truck over onto the side of the road. He jumped out, and then said, "Throw on your swimmers!" We obeyed his command and then followed as Paul led us through a dense patch of bushes. Eventually we popped out on top of a cliff that looked down over a crystal-clear river. Without any warning Paul jumped off the edge, splashing into the water fifteen feet below. Ryan and I followed suit and before we knew it we were back in the car zooming away from the secret little spot.

An hour later, Paul pulled the car over again, this time at a lake surrounded by the mountains. We swam with Paul to a tower in the middle of the lake that was at least twenty feet tall. Paul executed a perfect dive from the top, then Ryan and I jumped in after him. Then we were off again.

We arrived at the turnoff to Clearwater B.C. where Paul dropped us off on the side of the highway. We were going to go north to see some of Ryan's friends who were working on a farm. I stood there thinking about the fun drive we just had with Paul. I thought about the road trips I had taken before and realised that I was always focused on simply getting to my destination.

Not once had I ever stopped at a random lake or a river for a swim – I whizzed past them all. Paul had shown me that road trips weren't just about getting to your destination, but about enjoying the journey. I thought it was a perfect analogy for life. I realised that life wasn't about the destination, or retirement, or success. Instead, life was about enjoying each and every moment during the whole journey. Paul had unknowingly opened up my mind to a different way of thinking and for that I was thankful.

GOING NORTH
Kamloops, B.C. 3687 km.

"Wisdom defined is knowledge gained through experience."

We got a ride north in a pick-up truck from an old guy named Frank. The landscape was barren and empty and Frank explained that we were actually close to the Okanagan Desert. I was surprised to hear that we even had one. We drove through a valley covered in burnt trees.

"Last year there was a massive forest fire. Started from someone throwing a cigarette butt out a car window," Frank told us. "Thousands of acres were burned down." Eventually we left the burnt-out valley behind for beautiful evergreen trees and fields of lush greenery.

I reflected on our previous ride with Paul and I realised that he had wisdom, something that for the first time in my life I realised I lacked. My whole life had been filled with knowledge from books and teachers, but not experience from life. It seemed as though all the knowledge in the world was useless without any experience to back it up. My decisions were based on what I was told was correct, not on what I had experienced for myself. I realised that if I really wanted to be happy in life, I needed to gain more experience.

A few hours later we arrived in Clearwater, B.C. For the first time since I graduated university, I had an idea of what I wanted to do with my life and it was simply to gain more life experience.

LIVING ON A FARM
Clearwater, B.C. 3708 km.

"I'm a country boy wearing a city boy's clothes, I grew up in the city but the country is my home."

We walked over a bridge that took us over a raging river as we made our way into the little town of Clearwater. It was the smallest town we had stopped in yet with a population of around 2000 people. There were only a few shops, including a grocery store and the white-water rafting depot where Ryan's friends worked. We walked into the shop to see if they were around but they were out on the water.

We went back later in the day and found Ryan's friends unpacking wetsuits and paddles out of a big blue school bus. Ryan was stoked to see them and they greeted each other warmly. When they finished work, they drove us up to the farm where they were staying, which was a slow half-hour drive up the mountain.

At the top we pulled onto a property that had views of the mountains. There was a farm house, a couple of barns, and a tiny cabin. Once we were unpacked, we were given a tour by Eric and Josh. It turned out that they were farm sitting for the summer. The family that owned the property had gone on an extended fishing trip and had arranged for Eric and Josh to manage the place. In return they got free rent.

The farm had fifty sled dogs, all half-wolf and half-husky. They were all chained to wooden posts in rows with no room to roam. It was sad. When the dogs broke free, they viciously attacked each other frequently drawing blood. The farm also had cows, chickens, turkeys, and pigs. "You guys can stay as long as you want if you help with the daily chores," Eric assured us.

"I think I am going to get a job in town and stay on the farm for a while," Ryan said.

Again he caught me off guard with that comment. I thought we were on our way to the west coast. Thankfully, I had just learned that life wasn't just about the destination, but the journey along the way. I thought about it and decided that since I really had nowhere better to be, I would stay a few more days and if I liked it I would stay for longer.

Ryan and I moved into the tiny wood cabin at the end of the driveway. It had bunk beds, a sink, and the walls were lined with fragrant smelling cedar. The mosquitos were so bad around the cabin that every time we opened the door twenty more got inside. It was impossible to keep them out.

Each morning we ate breakfast, then we put on big rubber coveralls to feed the animals. We started with the dogs. We mixed buckets of food and water and when it turned into mush we filled the dog's bowls with it. We threw the chickens some grain and when they went to eat we snuck into their houses to collect all the eggs. To feed the pigs we mixed buckets of scraps from the local restaurant with water and dumped it in their pen. They would always have a bath in the rotten slop before they ate it and were clearly not at all concerned about what they were eating.

Ryan got a job working in the kitchen at the white-water rafting shop and I got a job painting at a resort that was being built just down the road. Every morning after feeding the animals I hopped on a bike and let gravity take me down the mountain to work.

The painting job was uneventful, but the picturesque mountains, the fresh air, and a view of the lake made every day enjoyable. After work one day some of the painters invited me to another lake for some beers. We drove to the bottom of the mountain to a pristine lake surrounded by lofty peaks. After we had a few beers the only boat in the lake pulled up to the shore and asked us if we wanted to go water skiing. The guys laughed at the request, but I gladly accepted it. Before I knew it, I was gliding across the glassy lake at full throttle. I was sure the guy was trying to make me wipe out, but I held on tight and enjoyed the ride while he sling-shotted me around the lake.

One day there were a few extra spots on a white-water rafting trip and the guys managed to get us in for free. We raced down the rapids bouncing around while holding on for our lives. Then halfway down the river, we parked our rafts and hiked to a waterfall that we took turns jumping off.

Time on the farm went by quickly and after a few weeks I decided that I was ready to move on.

"Hey man," I said to Ryan, "did you want to hitchhike to the ocean?"

"No, I think I might stay in Clearwater until the winter. But I was thinking of going to Mount Washington to do a season of snowboarding if you want to meet me there?"

The idea of snowboarding all winter sounded amazing, but when I researched Mount Washington it seemed to lack both affordable accommodation and work. But the idea intrigued me and I had heard of another mountain called Whistler not far away. I searched it on the ancient dial-up internet and was pleasantly surprised with the amount of opportunities and accommodation there. It even said it was the number one ski resort in North America. My mind was made up – I was going to ski in Whistler for the winter.

I was happy Ryan had led me to the farm, it had been a good experience and I learned how much work there actually is to do on one. It seemed as though it was never ending. I liked being around all the different animals, as they all seemed to have different personalities much like humans.

I planned a route to Vancouver on my laminated map of Canada. The thought of hitchhiking on my own was daunting, but it seemed like it was the only way I was going to get to the ocean. I picked a date of departure, packed my bags, and a few days later I hit the road alone.

ALL ALONE IN THE WORLD
Kamloops, B.C. 3831 km.

"The only person you are destined to be, is the person you decide to become."
—Ralph Waldo Emerson

Another comfort zone created and another comfort zone abandoned. Each time it was becoming a little easier to move on. I stood on the side of the road, alone with my belongings. I had the same feeling I had when Ryan and I first left to go hitchhiking a month earlier. That slightly guilty feeling that shows up when you think you're making a bad decision.

The road was quiet and lonely without someone to share it with. I felt as if I was waiting at a bus stop but there was no bus coming. Getting a ride was left to a split-second interaction between a stranger and myself. I sometimes wondered what people's reasons were for pulling over. As I stood there thinking about how I was going to get a ride, it occurred to me that the easier I made it for someone to pick me up, the higher the chance would be that I got a lift.

I had spent a lot of time on the farm reflecting on our journey. I had thought of making some rules for myself to follow when I hitchhiked with two distinct purposes. One to get a ride and the other to stay safe. Some of them I specifically created knowing I was going to be alone with strangers, aware that the risks are greater. Here are a few of them.

Hitchhiking Rules

1. Always stand where there is lots of room for a car to pull over.
2. Don't stand where the road is curved. There isn't enough time for a car to see you and decide if they want to pick you up, and it is a dangerous place for a car to stop.
3. Don't hitchhike on a hill. It's hard for a car to stop if they are driving downhill while it is annoying for them to stop if they are going uphill.
4. Try to stand where the speed limit is slower. If a car is already going slow, it isn't that much of an inconvenience for them to stop and start again. It is easier for a driver to see and judge you and still have time to pull over.
5. Never walk, just wait for a ride.
6. Don't accept drinks from strangers to avoid getting drugged.
7. Try to only travel the route planned. Or at least only

travel the route agreed on with the driver. If they change the plan, get out.

8. If you have a bad feeling, just say no to a ride or ask the car to stop and let you out.

9. Dress in brightly coloured clothing to stand out and to seem more appealing to drivers.

10. Play guitar or spin poi (fire) to look more interesting and less dangerous. This also attracts like-minded people.

11. Smile, look happy!

12. Don't accept offers of accommodation if the person doesn't seem honest.

13. Above all, follow your instinct.

I took a picture of the scenery on my old digital camera, then started the long wait on the empty road. I wondered if going off on my own was a good idea, but I knew only time would tell.

Not many cars went by that morning and the few that drove past didn't even look at me. I thought it was strange how some people didn't even look. But I suppose everybody has their own defence mechanisms, and what you don't acknowledge is easily forgotten. I realised that I had grown beyond my less experienced self that was desperate for a ride only a month before. I was in no rush to get anywhere because I knew it really didn't matter where I was. I had no place to be and no deadlines to follow – I was totally free.

A camper van pulled over that had an old guy named Jim behind the wheel. He was a music teacher on his way to a bluegrass festival with more instruments then I could count in the back. He had stopped because he saw my guitar and wondered if I was going to the festival as well. We chatted about music the whole ride and then he went out of his way and dropped me off in the middle of the city of Kamloops in B.C.

The hot Kamloops sun was unexpected and within minutes I was drenched in sweat. I trekked up the biggest hill I imagined any city could have while searching for my friend Shawn who was hosting a car show in town that day. I could hear music playing in the distance and was sure I had found my friend. But as I got closer, I realised I was just walking towards a car audio store. I decided to check it out anyways, just in case it was the right place.

I crossed the street to the welcoming smell of a barbecue; the parking lot was full of people and in the middle of a crowd there was a super car that looked like a spaceship. It must have had fifty speakers of all shapes and sizes surrounding its sole seat and my buddy Shawn was standing beside it. I walked up and said hi to him. It took him a second to realise that the sweaty, sun tanned, big bearded guy speaking to him was in fact me. When it clicked, he said, "oh Matt!"

"Hey man," I replied with a wide smile.

"You made it! That's crazy that you hitchhiked this far!"

"I know! I wasn't sure how it would go, but I'm still alive so that's reassuring!"

"Ha ha ha! All right, let's go get some drinks – I've got some Baileys in the truck."

"Sounds good to me."

We hopped in his truck and drove to a coffee shops drive-through, then drove off with some caramel macchiatos full of Baileys.

Once again, I was amazed at how quickly I went from feeling totally alone to feeling pretty comfortable just from meeting up with my friend. The feeling of loneliness seemed to all be in my mind. How I felt in a place seemed to be determined by how I perceived my surroundings and nothing more. It wasn't actually where I was that mattered, but how I felt about where I was that made me feel a certain way.

It became clear to me that if I wanted to grow as a person, I needed to change the perception I had of my comfort zone. I really didn't need a place or a person to make me feel comfortable. Did I? Surely I could learn how to feel comfortable with just myself, alone, anywhere. I decided to stop looking towards outside sources for the comfort that was surely always available from within.

Shawn and I went out for a nice dinner at a restaurant near his hotel, then walked back to his room and chatted about life. "The hotels got a water slide, eh?" Without hesitation we were doing laps of it like we were kids.

The next morning Shawn offered me a ride all the way to Vancouver. He was headed there for his next car show, the offer sounded amazing. A ride straight to the ocean! What more could I ask for? But I turned him down. My perspective had changed. I was no longer in a rush to get from point A to point B. Instead, I planned to meet up with some other friends on the way to the coast.

The next morning Shawn dropped me off on the side of the highway. It was hard to part ways with one of my good friends, especially under the circumstances. Part of what made it difficult was knowing that he was going across Canada as well, but in more comfort. He had money, a truck, he was getting paid, and had a home to go to after.

I couldn't explain to even myself what I was doing with no real plan. I had even studied strategic decision making in university. Yet there I was on the side of the highway, alone and staring off into the distance with no long-term plan. Wondering what I was doing with my life, while desperate for some sort of comfort zone. But who I was seemed more important than what I had at that moment. If I was going to grow as a person, I knew I had to take some chances.

A LITTLE TREAT
Vernon, B.C. 3947 km.

"The greatest fear, is the fear of the unknown."

It was easy to daydream on the side of the highway and once again I was lost in my thoughts, although I came back to reality pretty quickly when a black SUV pulled over.

"Hi, where are you headed?" I asked while looking over the occupants in the car. I only had a few seconds to decide if I was going to take the ride or not if it was offered, so I used them wisely. "We're headed to Vernon, B.C," the lady driving said. It was along the route that I wanted to go, so I accepted the ride and got in the empty back seat with my guitar and my backpack.

The lady driving was named Susan, while her husband Jack sat beside her.

"Where have you travelled from?" they asked as soon as we pulled away. I got out my map to show them, forgetting that I had recently used it to roll one up on. The leftover green crumbs were obvious, but they didn't say a thing about it.

One story led to another and before I knew it, we were in Vernon. "Is there anywhere in particular you want us to drop you off?" Susan asked.

"Nah, anywhere is good for me." She pulled into a parking lot on the edge of the highway and let me out.

Jack got out of the car and said, "I can give you a hand with your bags if you like." He helped me get them out from the back seat and I dropped them on the pavement. When I was ready to go, he said, "I have a gift for you in the back, but you aren't allowed to look at it until after we've left."

"Okay, sounds good to me," I said.

I wondered what it could possibly be and watched as Jack reached deep down into one of his bags. He pulled out a white grocery bag that looked empty, unzipped my bag, stuffed it inside and then did it up again with a grin on his face.

"Have a good trip," he said, then we shook hands and he got back in the car.

"Thanks for the gift and the ride, see you later," I said.

I watched as they drove off out of the parking lot and down the road. Before the gesture they already seemed like the nicest people, the gift just added to it.

I was eager to see what Jack had left in my backpack but decided to find a good hitchhiking spot first. I crossed the street and walked past the stop lights. There was no shoulder and no good place to stand, but I didn't really care. I looked around and saw that I was in the industrial area of Vernon. It wasn't a bad place to be, the grass was plush, and there were no bears to worry about if I didn't get a ride.

I unzipped my bag and wiggled my hand inside until I felt around for what Jack had put in there. When I opened it up, I was delighted to see a little bag of green crumbs, similar to the ones that were on my map.

Once again, I waited on the side of the road and watched people drive by. Some looked at me while others avoided eye contact. I wondered why I seemed to have a greater connection with the ones that met my eye, even if it was just for a second. It reminded me of something someone had once said to me that the only things that exist in your life are the things you put energy into.

FRIENDS AND FUN
Peachland, B.C. 4022 km.

"Don't count the days. Make the days count."
—Muhammad Ali

I was hoping to meet my friend Matt in Peachland B.C., which was only an hour from Vernon. He was flying in to visit his sister Laura, who I was also friends with, and he suggested that I meet them at her house. After half an hour on the road a middle-aged lady named Dianne picked me up. She was as nice as they come and we chatted the whole trip. She was a single mother on her way home from work. She invited me to her place for dinner but I declined, eager to see my good friends.

Dianne was kind enough to drop me at Laura's front door and I played her a song on my guitar before she left. "Hey Matt," she said looking out of her window at me, "If you ever change your mind about coming over for dinner, here's my number." She passed me a little piece of paper with her details on it.

"Thanks," I said.

"No problem," she replied, "the offer's always open and you can call me anytime." I shut the door, then waved as she drove off. It was nice to know that there were such caring people in the world.

I had arrived way earlier than expected, but I figured there was no harm in being there if Laura was around. When I looked up at the house, I was shocked by how big it was. It was also a lakefront property, but I figured that Laura had probably just rented a sweet house on the waterfront with her friends.

I knocked on the door and after a pause it was answered by an older lady named Madeline.

"Sorry, I must have the wrong address," I said before quickly turning around.

"Who are you looking for?" she quickly asked before I could get away.

"I was just looking for my friend Laura?"

"Well, you've come to the right place."

Laura wasn't home yet and I tried to get out of there, but the lady insisted that I waited for everybody else to show up. Sometime later and to my great relief Matt, Katie, and Laura arrived. We hugged, all super excited to see each other. They were like my second family.

They all wanted me to stay with them, and even Madeline didn't seem to care. But Madeline's husband Frank did not like the look of me. I just wanted to grab my bags and go camp in the bush. But when I suggested it to Matt, he laughed at the idea and said, "Just stay, who cares?"

in his usual light-hearted funny way. He was one of my good friends from university, a super intelligent guy who lived life by his own rules.

So at his insistence I stayed and the first few days were awkward. But once Frank and I had a good conversation and he realised I was polite and educated, I think he had a change of heart. To be fair, his initial reaction was warranted – I was a strange hitchhiker who had showed up to his house uninvited.

Peachland was a beautiful town on the edge of Lake Okanagan, which is a massive one hundred and thirty-five km long and five km wide freshwater lake surrounded by vineyards and orchards as far as the eye can see. The cold water had an inviting crisp blue hue.

One day we went wakeboarding in a boat that Laura was able to borrow. It started off perfect and one by one we took turns, then halfway through the day a strong wind started blowing and within minutes the calm lake turned into what seemed like a wild ocean. Waves battered the boat and we started to take on water. We turned on the pump and began to drain the ballast tanks but the water was coming in quicker than we could get it out. For a while it looked as though we were going to go down with the boat in the storm, but we made it to the dock at the last possible moment.

We spent the rest of the week exploring the town. On sunny days we floated down the lazy river on tubes, went paint balling, and hit the bars. At night we sat on the dock and watched shooting stars in the cloudless sky.

A week flew by and before I knew it I was in the car with

them on the way to the airport. When we reached my stop, Matt and his sisters dropped me off on the side of the highway. The looks on their faces showed a sadness that words cannot describe as they all struggled with the idea of leaving me there on the side of the highway. It was a sad goodbye and it was hard to watch them drive away down the highway and into the distance.

Just as quickly as night turns to day, I went from the highest of highs to the lowest of lows. Although I was getting used to being on the side of the highway alone, it was still hard to go from such an enjoyable situation with great friends and adventure to nothing at all. If the change had been gradual, it would have been easier to deal with. No house, no friends, and only the lonely road ahead of me. I had spent most of the money I had earned painting that week and was down to my last few hundred dollars.

Although I was lonely, I could feel that I was becoming more comfortable with who I was on the road. What the people driving by thought of me seemed to matter a lot less than it had a month earlier. I wasn't too worried about where I was going and tried to enjoy where I was. At the beginning of the trip the thought of being content with nothing was hard to grasp. But I was starting to understand that as long as I had food and water, nothing more was really necessary.

HITCHHIKING TO THE OCEAN

Peachland, B.C. 4022 km.

"The secret to happiness is freedom, and the secret to freedom is courage."
—Thucydides

I walked in the heat up the ramp towards Highway 97-C. The barren red landscape seemed to suck the moisture straight out of my skin. The orchards that surrounded Lake Okanagan seemed a world away from where I was now. Instead, sagebrush and cacti dotted the landscape. I stood waiting for a ride in the blistering hot sun while I dreamed of shade.

I had been rationing my water but it was now almost empty. Vancouver was starting to seem further away with every moment that passed even though there were many cars going by and most of them only had one lone driver. But it was not up to me who gave me a ride.

I spent the time contemplating my life. Who I was, where I wanted to be, and if any of that really mattered. To the cars going past I was a ghost. If there had been a lost dog on the side of the road, someone would have pulled over a long time ago. A reminder of the human condition.

A local farmer stopped and offered me a ride. He wasn't going far but I was glad to be going somewhere. He was named Tim and looked to be about sixty years old. The ride brought my spirits up and I didn't care if it was the only one I got that day.

A while later when I was back on the highway, an old white pick-up truck pulled over. A guy named Chris was driving and he looked like he lived on a farm too. His clothes were covered in dust, his truck had stained seats, and there was dirt covering the floor. The truck had a pungent smell and Chris looked like he hadn't showered for a few days.

We started off with the usual small talk before the conversation led itself into the good stuff.

"So what do you do for a living?" I asked

"Ha-ha, that's a funny question, I'm a grower," he said with a wink.

"Oh really?"

"Yeah, been doing it for years. Had a crazy week last week actually. I was just sitting at home and the cops knocked on the door. They said 'Chris, we have reason to believe that you are growing weed on your premises and we have a warrant to search the place.' So I said, 'yes officer, you're correct I am growing but I have a medical marijuana growing card so it's all legal. I have had the set-up wired by an electrician and I pay for my electricity, and as far as I know I am not breaking the law.'"

He got his medical marijuana growing card off the internet, which had absolutely no legal credibility, but he went with it.

"So, the cops said, 'oh, okay Chris, thanks for being honest, we'll tell you what we're going to do. We're going to give you the day to clean out all the plants and were going to come back tomorrow with an electrician to examine your operation.' Just like that they left. I spent the whole day moving out the plants and sure enough, the next day they showed up with the electrician. They looked over everything and then told me 'it's all good.' I haven't heard from them since. Crazy, eh!"

"Yeah man! I didn't expect your story to end like that, that's sweet!"

"I know! The plants are back in there now and everything seems to be fine."

As he was talking, I noticed something that looked like a crack pipe in the little space underneath the radio dials. I had only ever seen one on TV but it looked identical. I looked over at his glazed eyes and all of a sudden my situation seemed a whole lot sketchier.

The traffic on the highway slowed down but Chris maintained his speed, weaving in and out of cars like he was in a race. He was down shifting, up shifting, and revving the engine while whizzing past traffic with only inches to spare. Then when the whole highway slowed down to a stop, he took the off ramp at full speed without saying a word. One of the scenarios I had imagined before I set off on my adventure was happening to me – I was being taken away from where I wanted to go.

My heart rate sped up and I knew that I was breaking one of my hitchhiking rules. Sensing my uneasiness, Chris said "We're just taking a shortcut to bypass the congestion, we'll be back on the highway in no time." I was tempted to ask him to stop and let me out, but we were already far away from the highway and it would be a mission to walk back. To my relief, after a few kilometres he turned left and we began to drive on a road parallel to the highway in the same direction we had been going before.

The road we were on got closer and closer to the highway and we were able to see bumper-to-bumper traffic crawling slowly along it. "We got off right before the two highways joined into one," Chris explained. "There's always a traffic jam there, so I just go around it."

Before my thoughts ran too wild, we merged back onto the same highway as before. This time the cars were moving at full speed. We had bypassed the traffic jam and we were now driving along the Trans-Canada Highway straight towards downtown Vancouver.

When Chris arrived at his exit, he dropped me on the side of the off ramp. I was happy to be alone on the side of the road again instead of being with someone who made questionable life decisions. I looked down at the map and realised that I was almost halfway to Vancouver.

There was no on ramp to wait along after the off ramp and I was faced with the dilemma of how to hitch on the side of a major highway that had a hundred km/h speed limit. The cars were going so fast that they would have already passed by the time they noticed me. I stood in the small space that separated the edge of the highway from a chain-link fence. Beyond the fence a water treatment plant sent a strong smell of raw sewage into the air.

After an hour of waiting it started to rain and I hoped that perhaps it would encourage someone to stop and pick me up. But instead I just sat and waited in the rain instead of the sunshine. I didn't imagine that standing on the side of a wet highway was very safe, but I didn't know where else to go.

Eventually the traffic slowed down to a crawl, either because of rush hour or because of an accident, and a lady named Jess pulled over. She was pregnant, but said that she just couldn't drive past someone sitting in the rain. She was a really nice person and was kind enough to drive me for an hour until her turn off.

She dropped me off on the outskirts of Vancouver and the second I got out of the car I was engulfed by the sounds of the city. I thought of Ryan who I had left only a few weeks earlier, and imagined he was probably still sitting on the farm listening to all the dogs bark. I was nervous about arriving in Vancouver alone, but was still hoping to reach my goal of swimming in the ocean. I knew I wasn't far from successfully hitchhiking across Canada.

I hitchhiked along the on ramp certain that I would have better luck there rather than on the highway. Partly because the cars were going slower and partly because there was a bigger shoulder for them to pull over if they wanted to. I had only been on the side of the on ramp for ten minutes when a taxi pulled over. I went up to the window.

"Sorry, I wasn't waving you down," I said, "I'm just hitchhiking."

"Ha-ha, oh, I know," the Indian driver replied slowly and calmly with a large smile and a strong accent.

"Where are you going?" he asked.

"Downtown Vancouver."

With a chuckle, he said, "That could be anywhere my friend."

I showed him the address of my friend Jack.

"Oh, yes, I know the place. I'll take you near there. I've been working since very early this morning and would enjoy your company for the ride."

The man seemed very nice and I didn't hesitate to get in. "Thanks for picking me up. I had a long, rough day hitchhiking today in the heat and then the rain."

He said, "I noticed you looked a bit down and I thought maybe I'll give him a ride to make his day a bit better."

"Wow, thank you – I appreciate that." Just like that my faith in humanity was restored. One kind gesture can change the world.

"It is absolutely my pleasure," he said as we pulled into traffic.

The man introduced himself as John, but because he was obviously Indian, I asked, "What's your real name?"

"Ah, my friend, it's Ranjit."

We talked the whole way to Vancouver. Ranjit was wise

and full of great life tips. At one moment we passed a billboard just as it was changing and the new message said, 'Exactly where you want to be.' I took it as an omen. Sometimes the struggles in life happen for a reason. I knew that at that moment, on that day, everything had happened so I could talk to Ranjit and learn from him.

Ranjit drove me right up to the door of my friend's place in downtown Vancouver. "I was going this way anyway," he assured me, but I am certain he was just a really nice man that went out of his way for me. Someone I could learn a lot from.

I had already confronted a lot of my fears on the trip and felt that each day was getting a little bit easier. Perhaps the experience I had already gained was making me more comfortable in the situations I was facing each day. Such as being alone on the side of the road.

My stress that day was unnecessary. Instead of worrying I should have just relaxed and waited. Everything would have seemed easier and my day would have been more enjoyable. I knew that I needed to find more patience and to remember that wherever I end up is where I am supposed to be.

AS THE EAGLE SOARS
Vancouver B.C. 4402 km.

"It's not what you look at that matters. It's what you see."
—Henry David Thoreau

After being immersed in nature for the past few weeks, the soundtrack of the city made me feel like I had arrived somewhere I didn't belong. I looked around for a tree to get a glimpse of nature, but there were no trees to be seen in the concrete jungle I had arrived in.

I looked up at the sparkling windows of the high rise that seemed to rise into the heavens. I walked through the sliding glass doors and across the sparkling marble floor. I found Jack's name on the list of occupants, then buzzed his apartment with the anticipation of hearing his comforting voice, but there was no response. So I decided to go and find a pay phone to give him a call instead.

After a few blocks of searching I finally found one. I put the quarter in and dialled. Jack picked up after a few rings and we made plans to meet up later in the day. I could smell the saltiness of the ocean in the air, a strong but unfamiliar aroma. Evidence that I was close to the water, my goal, so I decided to go find it. After asking for directions, I started the long walk to the waterfront. Then for a moment I hesitated while I dwelled on the thought that perhaps it was too far to walk with my heavy bags. But then I remembered how far I had travelled, the struggles I had been through, the sacrifices I had made, and how much I had changed since I had left. Waiting was not an option.

I put my head down and pushed on, the smell of the ocean got stronger. I walked past shops and restaurants full of people. The city seemed alive with activity. Then before I knew it I heard seabirds squawking. My journey was near its end. I passed the last few restaurants on the block and I saw the Pacific Ocean for the first time. I crossed the street into Stanley Park and made my way onto the sandy shoreline.

An eagle soared above, a bird that symbolises strength and courage. I felt like a weight had been lifted off my shoulders. I couldn't understand why. Perhaps it was because I knew that the struggle was finally over. Once again I would integrate myself into the comfort of society's warmth. I would be accepted by those that now looked down on me. No longer would I be an outcast.

I dropped my bags on the sand and ran into the salty ocean. The water was freezing, but it was the reward I had earned for my persistence, so I enjoyed every salty drop on my skin. I couldn't believe that I had just hitchhiked across most of Canada. It was beyond my wildest dreams. I knew that I would never be the same again.

I was amazed at how content I was at that moment, alone in Vancouver with almost nothing to my name. I felt as if I had a lot more than I did when I left a few months before. I had food, water, and a place to sleep – all the necessities of life.

My friend Jack came to meet me after he finished work. We were friends from high school and it had been years since we had last seen each other. It was the first time that I had met up with a friend that I hadn't seen for years and I didn't know what to expect. To my surprise – Jack was pretty much the same person that I remembered and nothing between us seemed to have changed.

We ended up getting along really well, just like the old times. Originally I had only planned to stay a few days in Vancouver before I headed north for Whistler, but with each day that passed Jack invited me to stay for another. I made a point of being a good house guest. I left and explored the city during the day, and in the evenings I cooked dinner and cleaned up after us. Jack and I spent the sunsets on his balcony staring at the lights of the city and the mountains in the distance. There was something mesmerising about the place at night.

Stanley Park is the most beautiful place I had ever been to within a city. Encircled by the ocean, it is full of old growth trees with excellent views of the mountains. The park is always full of people walking, running, biking, swimming, kayaking, and busking. It was the total opposite of the parks that I grew up near back home. The park was alive!

Sometimes during the day I would wander into the

depths of the forest on my own to find a peaceful spot overlooking the ocean. I would spend the day meditating and playing guitar surrounded by the beautiful old-growth trees, with spectacular views of the ocean and the mountains. Each day I spent there, the city and the people that lived there grew on me.

I spent a lot of my time playing guitar on the street for money and along the way I met a lot of the homeless people that lived in the area. They seemed no different from me. Most of them had been contributing members of society their whole lives until some stroke of bad luck tipped them into oblivion. The loss of a job, a divorce, loss of kids, drug and alcohol addiction, mental health problems, and depression were a few of the reasons they ended up where they were. The list went on and their struggle was often a nightmare, unchecked and unnoticed by those who walked by. But most of them were good people, just down on their luck.

One day I was sitting alone on a rock in the ocean, surrounded by water, strumming away on my guitar. A homeless guy walked out onto the rocks and picked one beside me.

"Can I listen?" he asked politely while avoiding eye contact.

"Of course," I said.

He seemed nice, but a little edgy. He listened contently, then he pulled out a crack pipe and lit it up. I didn't know how to react and as quickly as he pulled it out, he put it away.

We chatted for a bit and when he had built up the confidence, he introduced himself as Elvis.

"I used to have a normal life," he said without me asking. "I had a job, a place – life was good, but then I tried crack and I have been on the street ever since. Can I play your guitar?"

I had to think about it for a second, but then I handed it over. I had a rule with my guitar. If anybody wanted to play it, they were welcome to. Music had given me so much, I was always happy to share it.

The thought crossed my mind that Elvis might run away with it, but I pushed it out of my head. I trusted him not to. I believe that trust earns trust. He fiddled with it for a bit, tuned it and strummed slowly with feeling, like a mother caresses her child. After another minute of fiddling around he got his groove on. Then he started to play face-melting renditions of Zeppelin, Hendrix, and Clapton with vocals too. Surely at one point in his life he must have been a successful musician.

It was early in the month of September and it was time to move on. I should have left before I ran out of money, but I had been enjoying my time with Jack. When I told him that I was going to leave for Whistler the next day, he offered to drive me there. So we left the next morning in Jack's black Mazda RX-7. The muffler roared every time he touched the gas. I was a bit sad to leave the city behind. While there I had realised that homeless people were normal folk just like me. I decided that I would make more time for them in the future, and try to help them out when I could. I had also learned that friendship was timeless. Even though I hadn't spoken to Jack for almost ten years, nothing had changed and we were still very good friends. I watched the old-growth trees of Stanley park fade away into the distance as we crossed the Lions Gate Bridge into the mountains.

The traffic thinned and the highway wound around tall jagged cliffs with a vertical drop of a thousand feet to the ocean below. The deep blue water of Horseshoe Bay met the majestic snow-capped mountains in the distance. Countless eagles soared overhead. I didn't know what to expect when I arrived in Whistler with no money, but I hoped that everything would work out for the best.

PARADISE FOUND
Whistler, B.C. 4524 km.

"If you live where you want to go on vacation, you will always be on vacation."

The entrance to Whistler had manicured green lawns and provided panoramic views of the mountains and ski runs. I had butterflies in my stomach, partly because I was excited to be moving to such a beautiful spot and partly because I knew I had no money or even a tent. It wasn't an ideal situation.

We drove through the village until we saw a sign that said 'staff housing.' There were seven buildings, and one of them had a reception sign out front. I walked down the steps and into the office. They were friendly and helpful and told me that even though I didn't have a job yet, I could still check in. However, I had to pay the damage deposit up front. To be honest I don't know how I had intended to get a place with no money. Regardless, my heart still sank. I realised that I should have spent the last of my money on a tent. I was not going to sleep outside in bear territory without at least a tent separating me from the creatures of the night. With no other option I swallowed my pride and asked Jack if he could help me out with the deposit, promising to pay him back as soon as I got a job.

It didn't faze Jack one bit and I walked out the door with a room key. I realised how alienated from society I had felt in the past two months and was excited at the thought of having my own room again. I walked into the building and up the grey stairs to the fourth floor. My apartment was number four hundred and seven and when I got inside I could see that I had an excellent view of the mountains from my bedroom. Jack came and checked out the room before he went back to Vancouver. I assured him that I would send him the money as soon as I had it.

I slowly unpacked my bag, happy to finally have a place to call my own again. I put up pictures of my friends and family on the walls, folded the few clothes I had away in the drawers and made the bed with the sheets they had given me. In the bottom of my bag I was lucky enough to find four dollars. It was the only money I had. In that instant my problems disappeared, aware that I was at least able to buy something to eat.

I appreciated having a place to call home again. I spent a lot of my time pondering life, trying to figure out how I should use the time I have been given on this Earth. Society had taught me how to get a job and how to sacrifice most of my time for money, based on the assurance that I can do anything in the world that I want when I retire. Yet there I was, sitting in the mountains, in the most beautiful place I had ever been, with no money and lots of time, doing whatever I wanted to do. It seemed surreal. I thought about how time was really all that anybody has in life. When it's gone, there is no more. It dawned upon me that time and effort can get me anything I want in the world, but nothing can get me more time. Which in a sense makes our time the most valuable thing in the world. I knew that my perspective of the world had changed quite a bit since I left home.

As each day passed, the temperature dropped and the snow started to fall. I got a job working for the Whistler Blackcomb ski resort in the employee services department, but my start date wasn't until November. I went to the local food bank to get something to eat each week until I got my first pay check. Once I got paid, it felt great to finally be able to go to the store to buy whatever I wanted. It was something I had missed.

My brother came to visit for a week. It was great to have him out in the mountains to show him the majestic wonderland that I had found. Within a few days he had already decided that he was going to fly home, sell all his stuff, and fly back for the winter. Two weeks later he returned.

It seemed as if most people had arrived in Whistler with bank accounts full of money and I was the odd one out. But I had my guitar, so I spent most of my time playing music at the lake. Time passed quickly and before I knew it opening day for the season was right around the corner. The whole town had a vibrant energy as the ski season approached and I started to wonder how I was going to get skis with no money.

Luckily, two days before the mountain opened I found out that Whistler Blackcomb employees were eligible for ski gear on credit. Payments would then get deducted from our pay checks, just like our rent was as long as our boss approved it. My bosses Heidi and Devon were kind enough to let me apply for credit.

I rushed to the ski shop on my lunch break to purchase some equipment. The shop had big glass windows and was full of people. After waiting to talk to a salesman, a guy with a beard and long hair walked up to me.

"Can I help you with anything?" he asked.

"Yeah, I was hoping to get this pair of skis and these bindings on credit with Whistler Backcomb."

"Cool, that we can do. Did you want us to put the bindings on them for you?"

"Yes, please!" I replied excitedly, dreaming of powder runs on the first day. "Can you have them ready by opening day?"

"Ha ha ha dude, not a chance. See that pile of skis over there?" he said as he pointed to the back room packed full of them. "Those all need bindings and they are all ahead of your skis. We could probably have them done within a week."

"Hmmm, what if I pay you extra? Do you accept tips?"

"Sorry dude, I would love to help but it's just not possible."

"Do you like beer?"

A smile broke out on the guy's face.

"Yeah, I like beer," the salesman replied.

"What's your favourite kind?"

"Heineken's pretty good."

"Cool man, I have got to go. What time are you working till?"

"Five today."

"All right, I'll be back."

I walked to work, wondering if my plan was going to work. The conversation hadn't gone that far, but I didn't want to push it. I think that his smile had said enough. When I finished work, I grabbed a cold twelve pack of Heineken and went back to the ski shop.

"Hey man."

"Hey dude, you're back," the same salesman said. I saw his eyes briefly take a glance at the case of beer I was holding. I handed it over.

"I got you some beers, I thought you might like them."

"Thanks, I appreciate that. Tell you what, come here at six pm the night before the mountain opens and your skis will be ready."

I smiled, we shook hands, and parted ways. Two days later at six in the evening I picked up my skis as arranged.

Opening day was a spectacle. The line-ups for the lifts were long and filled with people dressed up in costumes and funny ski suits. I waited in line with my roommates while we watched the gondolas slowly climb the mountainside. I was nervous. I had been up to the top before it had snowed, the mountain peaks and ski runs were the biggest and scariest that I had ever seen. But nobody seemed scared. I reassured myself that there was nothing to be afraid of.

When we finally got to the front of the line, the ski attendant scanned our ski passes while they checked that the pictures matched our faces. I walked awkwardly closer to the lift in my clunky ski boots. All my other friends were on snowboards and I was the odd one out. But I grew up skiing, so I figured I knew what I was doing. We crammed into the gondola with some strangers, there was no room to spare. The lift swung off the platform and into the air. It climbed the mountain in between a row of evergreen trees dusted in snow. Every time it swung, vibrated, or jerked to a stop, my heart raced, scared that something had gone wrong.

Eventually, the gondola crawled to a stop and the doors opened, but nobody got out. I wondered why, but it turned out that we were only halfway up the mountain. The doors closed again and the ascent continued. We rose above the clouds, and it felt as if we had gone into the heavens, after a while we reached the top of the mountain. We stepped out into fresh snow while people rushed to get down the slopes as if all the snow was going to run out. I put on my skis, my friends strapped on their boards, then we began the descent through the perfect soft powder. When I fell, the snow was fluffy and forgiving although it seemed to find its way into all the tiny nooks and crannies of my body. Each run we went down gave us different views of the surrounding mountain peaks sticking up through the clouds. I knew I had arrived in paradise.

The Whistler-Blackcomb ski resort is made up of two mountains and over 8000 acres of skiable terrain accessed by almost forty ski lifts. With almost two hundred ski runs designed for all abilities and restaurants up and down the mountain there is a reason it is one of the best ski resorts in North America.

Each day that I wasn't working, I went skiing with my friends and each day that we rode, we got a little better at riding while we explored a little more of the mountains. A typical day consisted of getting up, skiing down to the village, getting a banana smoothie, and then taking the lift up to the top. Then we would pick a run. Sometimes when the conditions were perfect we would do the same run over and over. If it was icy, we would go down the race courses as fast as we could, if it was a powder day we would go to the bowls or the tree runs. If we got hungry we would go and get some food at one of the mountain's restaurants. The amount of people we were with each day always grew as friends who had slept in eventually came and joined us on the mountain.

Some days we would bring backpacks full of beer, snacks, and a speaker up the mountain and we would build a ski jump wherever the views were the best. We would spend the whole day taking turns going off the jump, drinking beer, and enjoying the majestic scenery. When we had snacks, Whiskey Jack birds would fly in and eat out of our hands.

After long days of skiing we would go to the Crystal lounge or Cheetas bar for twenty-five cent wings, nachos, and pitchers of beer. A harmless drink after a good day of skiing. But more often than not we would end up in the bars a lot longer than we had anticipated. When a good time was being had it was easy to end up in your full ski gear at eleven pm. Somebody would suggest going out to dance and whoever was still in their ski gear would be forced to make a decision between going home and changing, or going out to the club in a coat and ski gear. Quite often more than a few people ended up in the club, ski gear and all.

The building I lived in was like residence in university except that nobody had homework or deadlines. Parties flourished, travellers met the loves of their lives, and shenanigans occurred on a daily basis. But everybody knew that they were only allowed to live in their accommodation because of their job. Sleeping in was not an option and those that lost their jobs also lost the room they slept in.

Quite often we would get beers and sneak into the hot tub of one of the many fancy resorts that Whistler had to offer. Most hotels had an outdoor hot tub that was easily accessed by jumping a fence or climbing a wall. Other times guests would give us the key cards to their rooms after they checked out, allowing us to get into the hotel's facilities at least for the night before the cards expired.

Whistler was a place where who you knew was more important than what you had. If you wanted to get into the bars you had to know the bouncers, if you wanted free shots you had to know the bartenders, if you wanted free food you had to have friends in the restaurants and ideally something to give back. Low wages and a high living cost seemed to create a system of bartering that I had seen nowhere else in my life. Everybody seemed to help each other out.

It seemed that every day in Whistler got a little bit better than the day before and the longer I stayed the more I felt at home. Everything seemed perfect in Whistler almost like nothing could ever go wrong.

DEATH COMES LOOKING FOR ME
Whistler, B.C. 4524 km.

"it is easy to not appreciate something until you almost lose it."

When I was standing on top of the mountain, I felt like I was on top of the world. I had risked it all on my journey in search of something greater and I knew I had found it. Time, freedom, friends, and snow – a magical mix. Every morning when I woke up to ride, I put on a song by The Ark's called One of Us is Going to Die Young. I just loved the infectious beat that pumped me up for a day of skiing. But perhaps I was singing the wrong lyrics because it wasn't long until the words caught up with me.

It started as just another powder day on the mountain. I took the chair lift up with a crew of my buddies like normal, but most of the guys wanted to do park laps. I was more interested in powder runs, and my buddy Jeff said he knew some that were loaded with powder. It sounded like another one of my dream days. Jeff was an expert skier and I followed him blindly, trusting that he wouldn't take me anywhere too far beyond my ability. We took the ski lift to the top of the mountain and traversed to the sun bowl. It was close to many of the spots I had skied before so nothing seemed amiss.

We arrived at the beginning of the run, but I couldn't see very far down it. It was steep, but a lot of the runs were steep at the beginning, so I didn't think anything of it. The sun was high and there wasn't a cloud in the sky. We passed two ski patrollers and I heard one say to the other, "over equipped and under experienced." I wondered if they were talking about us, and if so, why?

I followed Jeff as he slid sideways down the steep slope. As we continued it got steeper and icier and my heart began to race. We traversed past rocks and zigzagged back and forth as we descended towards the run. I looked up at the icy path we had taken and I thought to myself that there was no way to get back up, the only way to go was down. All I could see below us were rocks with small pockets of snow in between them. I was scared but Jeff reassured me everything would be all right and for some reason I trusted him.

"Watch my line closely and take the same one," he said before he began his descent. He got one turn and then another, but things didn't go as planned. I watched as he lost control and slid down the icy chute. He then flew off a small cliff and started tumbling uncontrollably head over heels. I watched in horror, scared that he was going to be seriously injured. But he eventually tumbled to a stop. He stood up and waved his ski poles at me.

I considered going back up, but it was too icy and too steep. I knew there was no way I could climb back up without slipping and tumbling all the way down. I thought that perhaps if I went slowly I would be all right. Jeff was still waving his ski poles up at me so I figured that meant it was my turn to go. I went slowly and took the first little drop which wasn't too bad. I got one more turn in before both my skis started sliding on the ice and I lost control.

Before I knew what was happening, I was sliding down near vertical ice. My skis connected with the first of many rocks, they stopped for just a second, then hurtled me violently over the ledge. When I next hit the ground, both my skis were torn from my feet. I started tumbling faster, head over heels, smashing all parts of my body on the rocks as I went. Everything turned into a blur. My hat, goggles, and gloves flew off, and my ski poles disappeared. I tried to cover my head as I crashed into countless rocks, but the momentum kept my arms away from my head. Eventually I started to slide and all that was left was snow. The ground levelled out and finally I came to a stop.

All I could think when I stopped was that my back hurt. It hurt a lot. What was wrong with my back? I wondered. I touched it with my hand and my suspicions were confirmed that it hurt. My hip hurt, my face hurt, my legs hurt, and my arms hurt. But my back, I kept thinking about it because my back *really* hurt. I looked up at Jeff and he said, "Are you okay man?"

"I don't know, my back hurts. Can you look at it?"

I lifted up my coat and showed him. All the colour instantly drained from his face until he was as white as the snow.

I asked him, "How does it look?"

He stuttered.

I knew it was bad, it wasn't so much the pain, but how it felt – something felt very wrong.

Jeff said, "Should we call patrol?"

We were far away from them and I didn't want to wait. I told him to grab my skis, I had a feeling I needed to go to a hospital.

Jeff ran up the mountain and grabbed one of them, then ran higher and grabbed the other. He was taking too long. He ran the skis to me, and I looked at the bottoms, they were shredded and most likely garbage. My face was bleeding; my shirt was covered in blood.

"Get my ski poles too! Actually, screw it – give me yours and let's go!" I was sure that time was of the essence.

The next section of the mountain was covered in icy moguls. Each one I skied over shot pain through my entire body. I told myself to suck it up, if I could just make it to the hospital everything would be okay. We arrived at the bottom of the run where we had to traverse for a kilometre to the lift. We had to go up first so we could get to a run that would take us to the village. The traverse was flat and slow and my shredded skis weren't helping. I watched as person after person passed me, they all asked if I was okay. Jeff raced ahead and left me on my own. It pissed me off, I figured the least he could have done was stayed with me. I felt alone.

My god, I thought to myself, what did I do? Why had I just blindly followed someone into danger? It was what we all did every day. The frustration was replaced with pain as I struggled to make any distance on my ruined skis. Finally, I saw the Harmony Chair lift line ahead where Jeff was waiting. When I saw his face, I realised he was probably in as much shock as I was and that he wasn't thinking very clearly.

Perhaps it was the adrenaline, but for some reason we just went and waited in line with everybody else as the blood flowed out of my back. When we got to the front of the line, my roommate Derek was operating the lift. I showed him my back and then hopped on the lift. He turned white too.

Halfway up the lift I started to feel nauseous.

"Can you put the safety bar down?" I asked, "I'm not feeling so good."

Jeff put it down and I held on tight. I didn't yet know the extent of my injuries and I felt as if death was knocking on my door. We got off the lift and traversed to the ski patrol hut. I walked in to the office and a few patrollers looked up at me from their conversation.

Their faces lit up and one of them said, "Oh, hi Matt, to what do we owe the pleasure?" I knew a lot of the patrollers from my employee services job, most of them by name. I didn't want to freak them out too much, so I casually said, "oh, not too much, just got a little cut on my lip," which I'm sure they would have already seen by then.

One of the patroller's said, "all good Matt, just head into the room over there and someone will be in to look at it." I don't remember which patrollers were there but I walked past them into the medical room and sat down on one of the beds. A patroller came in and asked me what was wrong. I told her as I lifted up my jacket, she looked shocked and then she ran out of the room.

Two more patrollers ran in, they took my coat off and laid me down on the bed. "Where did you do this? How did you get back to patrol? How do you feel? Are you nauseous? Can you see straight?" One after another I was drilled with questions. The patrollers left the room.

I stood up and walked to the mirror. I turned around to look at my back, and saw that there were two huge gashes and one had a long piece of skin hanging off of it. I tensed up and almost fell over as the reality of the situation hit me. It was no joke. I felt the blood leave my face, I felt dizzy, I looked away from the mirror, and grabbed onto the side of the bed. I spun myself around and then lay down on my stomach.

I was silent. I didn't want to talk to anybody anymore. What had I done to myself? Did I just blow it all because of some silly hitchhiking trip? Because I wanted to see what was out there? Was I going to die? Had I permanently injured my internal organs? Terrible thoughts rushed through my head. All of a sudden everything in my life seemed so insignificant, so petty. I didn't realise it until that moment, but my body was the most important thing I had in life. I thought time was, but with no body to experience it, time doesn't exist.

"How are you doing Matt?" a patroller asked. "The doctor

will be here shortly, then we will send you to the hospital if he thinks you are okay to get there."

"I'm all good," I lied.

I put my face back down on the bed. Time seemed to stand still. It felt as if the doctor was never going to arrive. The blood was trickling out of my back at a steady rate. I could feel it leaking out of me.

Finally, the doctor walked into the room. I felt slightly relieved. He looked at my wounds and asked me some questions. He looked into my eyes with a light. Then he covered the injury with some gauze and bandages.

I heard him say, "He's okay to go to the hospital now, it looks like he got pretty lucky."

The patrollers escorted me out of the patrol hut and onto a snowmobile. We drove to the top of the ski lift where another patroller was waiting for me. She led me into a gondola and we rode to the bottom of the mountain. When we got there a truck was waiting to take me to the hospital.

After a quick ride, I walked through the cold and into the hospital waiting room. It was full of injured people. Some people were clutching their arms, others their legs, everybody was in pain. With the waiting room already full, it didn't look like I was going to get in to see a doctor any time soon. The woman at reception told me to go and have a seat at a nurse's station.

I walked over and sat down, a nurse walked up and asked, "Can you show me all your injuries please?" I took off my shirt and showed her the large laceration that ran down my back and then the large hole the size of a fist that was beside my spine. One by one I pointed to each spot on my body that hurt and I told her why. She wrote down every injury and then said, "All right, now go have a seat in the waiting room, your name will be called on the loud speaker when we are ready for you." I had just found a seat when I heard my name being called.

Everyone's eyes in the waiting room turned towards me as I slowly got to my feet. I walked past them and through the doors into the emergency department. A nurse greeted me and led me into a private room. She then took off my jacket, sweater, and shirt before she told me to lie down on the bed.

"A doctor will be along shortly," she assured me.

I had only been on the bed for a minute, but there was already a pool of blood beside me and it was getting larger every second.

A doctor walked in and said, "How are you doing Matt? That's one of the worst lacerations I've ever seen." Then two more doctors walked in to inspect my wounds. I didn't know if having three doctors show up almost immediately was a good thing or a bad thing. Only time would tell.

They all started prodding and poking me. I could feel them stick their fingers inside the bloody holes on my back. They poked around inside my body as they tried to assess the damage. It felt horrible.

"Okay, were going to have to get you to pee in this cup, then were going to send it off for analysis. When the results come back, we will know if you need to be airlifted to Vancouver or not."

I laid back down on the bed and watched the nurse wipe up the first pool of blood. Then I watched as more blood filled in the void.

A while later, the doctor came back and said, "You're a lucky man Matt, you could have ruptured your kidney. It has experienced some trauma, but it looks like today is your lucky day. You narrowly avoided death, so you should take that as a lesson."

After the doctor left, the nurse led me through the corridor where she ushered me in and out of different rooms where they gave me various scans and x-rays.

I thought about what the doctor had said about narrowly avoiding death. It was true and I was indeed lucky. My injuries could easily have been fatal.

When the rest of the test results came back the doctors were surprised.

"It looks like you were extremely lucky today," another said. "Besides the flesh wounds, you somehow managed not to injure yourself too badly. You should count your blessings."

I couldn't keep track of who was talking when I was lying face down, but someone said, "Okay Matt, I'm going to give you some needles to freeze everything and then were going to put you back together again."

The doctor stuck needle after needle into my back, but I lost count after twenty jabs. When he was satisfied, he poked up and down my back with his finger and asked, "Does that hurt? Does that hurt? Does that hurt?" repeatedly, until he was sure that everything was frozen.

"Okay, now I am going to start stapling you back

together, let me know if it hurts and I can freeze it some more."

The first twenty-two staples were okay, but when he hit twenty-three I winced in pain and the doctor stopped. He put some more of the freezing agent into my back, then put the last five staples in resulting in a total of twenty-seven. That sealed up the long laceration that ran down my back.

Then he moved into the gaping hole that was right over my kidney. It took a lot longer to fix that. I imagined that it was like trying to sew up a hole in a T-shirt. He put fourteen stitches in before he was happy. Then he put two stitches in my lip to close that wound.

"There you go!" he said happily when he finished, "you're as good as new!"

The nurse came in and put bandages over the wounds and then sent me on my way. When I walked out of the emergency room, I was happy to be alive. My boss from work was waiting for me when I walked out of the door. It was nice to see a familiar face. Thoughts flooded my head. What if the hole in my back was an inch to the right? My spine would have been ripped in half. The cut on my lip could have been a rock that smashed my face in. I walked slowly through the village with Devon and we watched the snowflakes fall. Everything looked beautiful with the fresh layer of snow as if we were walking through a winter wonderland. The thick drifts muffled the sounds of the village and everything seemed so peaceful.

The snow crunched each time I took a step. I thought about how close I had come to dying. It wasn't the first time in my life that had happened, but this time it really shook me up. But I decided not to dwell on it. I cleared my mind and got back into the moment where I was alive, happy, and well, besides the throbbing pain in my back.

When I arrived at my apartment most of my friends showed up one after the other to see what I had done to myself. They all freaked out when I showed them. For some reason, everybody seemed a lot more concerned than I was. It wasn't until I saw the look on my brother's face that the reality of the situation hit home.

I tried showering the next day, but it was too painful. So I decided to wait until everything healed before I showered again. A few days later I woke up in the middle of the night in pain, it hurt to move and felt as if a stitch was stuck to my bed sheet. When I rolled over I felt it rip out, then a little pool of blood formed on the bed. I probably wasn't going to get my deposit back for the bloodstained sheet. Each day the pain seemed to get a little worse, but I figured it was because my wounds were healing.

My bosses Devon and Heidi questioned me about my recovery almost every day. When I finally admitted that it hurt more, they demanded to see my wounds. I didn't want to take the bandages off, but they insisted. They both looked shocked when they were removed.

"It's infected Matt! You need to go to the hospital immediately," they demanded.

"Okay, I'll go when I finish today," I replied.

"No, you're going to go now! You're not allowed back to work until you go!"

"But I really need the hours," I protested.

"Look Matt, you can die from an infection. If you don't go now, it might be too late. You've got to take this seriously."

I trudged through the slush towards the hospital. When I got there, the wait was long. The nurse repeated the same thing that my bosses had told me. She cleaned my wounds and then redressed them. Before I left, she said, "You are going to have to come back every day for at least the next week to have your wounds cleaned out. The only time of day we can spare extra time is at seven in the morning before the mountain opens. So you are going to have to be here every day at that time. If you choose not to listen to me, this infection could spread to your bloodstream and you could die from blood poisoning. Please take this seriously." Finally, after a week of early morning trips to the hospital, I was told that they finally had the infection under control and that once again I was lucky to be alive. I thanked Devon and Heidi for looking out for me and was thankful that they were in my life.

When I finally started skiing again I did so with a new appreciation for my life and my body. As the season continued everybody eventually took their turn in the hospital with broken arms, legs, backs, and everything in between. It was just part of the game; some learned from their mistakes and some didn't.

Over the next few months we were blessed with almost unlimited powder days. The parties got better, our crew got tighter, and every day was the best day of my life. Spring riding was one of my favourite parts of the season. The temperature went up, the sun shined brightly in the deep blue sky, and by noon the snow became soft and playful. My friends and I spent our days on the mountain just messing around and having fun. We spent days building jumps and drinking beers while enjoying the amazing views only available from the top of the mountain.

The ski season wrapped up nicely and one after another people left town to go back home. Others decided that they were never going to leave. That ski season gave me more than I ever imagined I could get out of life and it left me with a new appreciation for living. I felt content and successful, not because of the amount of money I had in my bank account, but because of the smile that was on my face before I went to bed every night. I no longer desired money, cars, or fancy clothes. Instead I wanted to live every one of my days to its fullest. I realised what a success my hitchhiking journey had truly been. It had led me to a life that I otherwise would have never thought existed. I had learned a way to live away from the city and its stress. It was a different way to exist.

The mountains were so big that even after exploring them all winter long I had only made a small dent in the almost unlimited terrain. The snow melted, summer arrived, and my thirst for new adventure grew. I knew that the path of my life was changed forever. I learned that if I picked my life wherever I wanted to be, I could fit a job in the cracks and every day could be spent living the dream. Most importantly I had learned that if I lived where I wanted to go on vacation, I would always be on vacation.

ON THE ROAD AGAIN
Tofino, B.C. 4524 km.

"Do you want to be safe and good, or do you want to take a chance and be great?"
—Jimmy Johnson

It was the beginning of May, my winter had been a dream come true and I was hoping for a summer full of adventure like the one I had the year before. My brother stayed in Whistler while my sister Nicole flew across Canada and met me in Tofino, a small surf and fishing town on the west coast of Vancouver Island. Besides a grocery store, a bar, and a few restaurants scattered around near the docks, Tofino was a quiet place with a mellow vibe and a small population of less than 2000 people.

I hadn't seen my sister since I had left to go hitchhiking the summer before and it was great to catch up with her. She was petite with long brown hair, and we had always got along well. A year earlier she had become so intrigued by my hitchhiking adventures she had decided that she was going to try it too. I had told her that the road was dangerous and that if she had to go, I would prefer that she went with me, knowing that I would do my best to keep her safe. We had a vague plan made to hitchhike to a festival in the middle of British Colombia, but it wasn't for a while. We spent our first week in Tofino exploring the beaches and the ocean and at night we camped in the bush. One day when we were sitting at the beach a van packed full of surfers pulled up beside us.

They had more than ten surfboards strapped to the roof and when they got out, I noticed that one of the guys was a friend of mine from Whistler so I went and said hi.

"Eric! How's it going man?"

"Good dude! I've just been living in Tofino and surfing. Life is good."

"Nice man, where are you living?"

"I live on a farm. Actually, I'm a woofer there."

"A woofer? What's that?" I asked, as I had never heard the term before.

"Oh, it's when you live on a farm and work for food and accommodation. It's a pretty sweet deal, mainly because they have surfboards we can use."

"That sounds sick! Where do I sign up?"

"Well, if you want to surf I can just ask Doug, he lets anybody use his boards."

"Dude, that would be amazing!"

My friend introduced me to Doug and after a little chat he offered me a board and wetsuit to use. Getting into the wetsuit was a challenge all on its own as it seemed so small and tight. But after some wiggling, I managed to get it on. I grabbed the nine-foot surfboard and walked towards the water's edge. Surfers were catching waves in what seemed like the middle of the ocean. I planned to do the same. I dropped the board in the water and crawled on top of it. The water was ice cold and seemed to seep through the wetsuit. I began the long paddle out to the rest of the surfers. I had only gotten twenty feet away from the shore when the first wave hit. It smashed me off the board and rolled me under the water like I was inside a washing machine. Well, I thought as I was getting back on the board, I had better go over the next one. But the next one smashed into me too. I battled the waves, trying with all my might to get further out, but the waves didn't stop coming. Eventually I accepted that I was just going to have to try surfing where I was. I ended up getting a few quick rides that were fun. Surfing was way harder than I had imagined it would be.

I walked back onto the beach. My feet were frozen and I couldn't feel my toes. They were numb and not responding to my brain's impulses to move. But apparently that is a normal day in the life of a surfer.

I was exhausted and was quite happy to just relax. The rest of the surfers from the van had started a campfire on the beach and I was content to bask in its warmth.

Doug invited us to the farm with the promise of food, a place to camp, and the use of the surfboards in return for a few hours of work per day. It sounded like a great deal. After we watched the sun set at the beach we followed Doug down a long dirt road into the sticks.

THE ORGANIC HIPPIE
LETTUCE FARM
Ucluelet, B.C. 4524 km.

"Finding an opportunity is a matter of believing it's there."
—Barbara Corcoran

The next morning I got my first good view of the farm. It was at least two acres with only a small section designated for growing lettuce. Tents, campers, and vans were scattered around the rest of the land. They were the homes of the people that lived there.

We woke up to breakfast already made for us at six in the morning. Then we tended to the lettuce patch for a few hours. The farm had at least twenty-five people working and staying there. Some of them picked fresh lettuce, while others planted lettuce or fertilised the organic gardens with fish guts. After we finished the daily chores everybody ate a big lunch together, then we packed the van with the boards and lettuce. Most days we delivered the lettuce to local restaurants on the way to the ocean.

One day when we were at the beach, two French Canadian girls showed up. Doug used the same technique with them that he had used on us. It all started with some surfing and then he would bring them back to work. It was smooth, and a great deal for all involved.

The French girls put on some wetsuits and went into the water. Since there were no single girls on the farm, I decided it was an ideal moment to get to know them before the rest of the guys introduced themselves. So I put on a wetsuit and headed into the water to help them surf.

"Hey, do you girls want a bit of help?"

"Oui, merci," they both answered in French.

They turned out to be sisters from Quebec with beautiful French accents. Jennifer was brunette with a voluptuous body and nice long hair while her sister was a little younger and blonde. I pushed them into waves and taught them the little that I knew until they were exhausted. When we got back to the parking lot, Doug invited them to the farm and they accepted the offer.

A few days later we went to see a reggae band at a local bar. After the show we all ended up drinking around the campfire back at the farm. I got my guitar out and played some songs, then I noticed that Jennifer had taken a seat beside me. After a few songs, she started rubbing my leg. I was surprised, but didn't object. Then as the night progressed, she started twisting the side of my shorts into a ball until the seams dug into my leg. I made eye contact with her and she twisted my shorts even tighter.

"Do you want to go for a walk to look at the stars?" I asked her. She grabbed my hand without answering and we walked off into the darkness. Alone, we looked up at the stars and I played a song for her. Then she leaned in and kissed me. We cuddled and enjoyed the warmth of each other's bodies in the cool evening air. After a while we went back to my tent.

The next morning when Doug gave the wakeup call, not one person got up. This was mainly due to the fact that everybody was so hungover from the whiskey that Doug had bought everyone the night before. We decided to abandon the farm for the day. Doug became upset and raised his voice, desperate to get people to do the work, but not a single person budged. The restaurants expected the lettuce delivery by the early afternoon but it didn't look like anybody was going to help. The whiskey had taken its toll and unfortunately that infuriated Doug. Jennifer and I spent the morning cuddling.

We decided while listening to Doug yelling at everybody that it was time for us to leave the farm. Just like the others that came and left on an almost daily basis we to would be only a brief memory in the minds of the people that we had met. We packed our bags, said goodbye to everybody, and then left the farm with no plans to return.

Living on the farm had made me realise how much I missed hitchhiking and meeting new people on the road. Jennifer reminded me how much I had missed the touch of a woman. But sometimes when you stop looking for what you want, what you want comes looking for you.

A TRIP
Tofino, B.C. 4524 km.

"A large part of life's journey is within ourselves, not in the material world."

We had been hanging with an older guy named John since our first day in Tofino. He was wise and kind, so when he invited us to go out to his cottage for the weekend, we gladly accepted his invitation. The cottage was a half-hour boat ride away from town and we had made plans to meet him at the dock.

My sister along with the French girls and I jumped into John's little boat and he steered off through the glassy water in the inlet. Then when our course was set, John poured everybody drinks. We cruised past countless islands while listening to reggae music. The scenery in the distance was reflected on the water. Colourful pink, purple, and white lily pads bloomed on the water. After a while we reached a secluded beach.

We transferred our gear from the boat into a canoe and

paddled to the shore. "Start a fire and set up your tents, I'll be back in a bit," John said, then he disappeared into some bushes.

The beach was a few hundred metres long with rocky outcrops at both ends. I couldn't quite tell if we were on an island or connected to the mainland, but it didn't really matter. We set up our tents and started a fire just as John arrived with some snacks. We relaxed in the sand and enjoyed the view of the mountains in the distance.

John gave us a tour of his off-grid cottage. It had everything that a normal house would have including running water, heating, electricity, and an outdoor washroom. The washroom was a short stroll from the house through an old-growth forest. A toilet and sink sat on top of a deck that was built in the centre of three old-growth trees, there were no walls or roof. It was the most beautiful bathroom I had ever seen. Then John showed us a sauna he had built in the woods.

"If you chop up some wood, we can have one after dinner," he said.

I spent a few hours chopping wood until dinner and then we lit a fire in the sauna. When it was hot enough, we walked through the dark woods and into the small wooden structure where we were welcomed by the strong smell of cedar. We had been feeding the stove with wood all evening and it was extremely hot. Once everybody was sitting comfortably, John dumped the first scoop of water on the fiery hot stove and a cloud of steam filled the room.

The steam spread quickly while John continuously

dumped water on the stove. In seconds the sauna went from being mildly warm to unbearably hot. I breathed slowly while I tried to get used to the extreme heat. "If you're too hot, go jump in the ocean," John said.

We left the sauna and made our way back down the path to the beach. We spent the rest of the evening running back and forth from the sauna to the ocean; it was a magical way to spend the time. After three days at Johns we ran out of supplies. The next day he dropped us off at the docks where he had picked us up.

Going out to John's off-grid home gave me a whole new perspective of how to live a simple but happy life. He had all the amenities of a normal house but without the mortgage or bills. It showed me that there was a way to live the minimalistic life with freedom while still having the luxuries of our modern world. I dreamed of living in a little shack in the woods just like his.

POOLE'S LAND

Tofino, B.C. 4580 km.

"When you have more than you need, it is easy to appreciate having very little."

The French girls left town to go cherry picking in the Okanagan Valley. It was sad to see them go, but I was glad that we had met. Without any obligations to be anywhere, my sister and I just hitchhiked around and explored the area. That was until a ride told us about a hippie commune called Poole's Land.

They were going past the place so we got dropped off at the driveway of Poole's Land to see what it was all about. It was a fifteen-minute walk from the Tofino shops so we figured if we didn't like it we could just walk to town. My sister and I walked up the sandy lane past all sorts of tropical plants that I had never seen before. At the end of the driveway there was a little house. When we knocked on the door a tall grey-haired man greeted us with a smile and a gentle voice. His name was Mike Poole.

"Hi," he said, looking at us inquisitively.

"Hi, how are you? We heard we might be able to work in return for accommodation here?" I replied.

"Oh, I'm sorry, I don't need anybody else at the moment."

"Oh, okay," I replied, "thanks anyway." We turned around and started to walk away, visibly disappointed.

"Actually, you know what?" Mike called out after us. "I might have some work after all. Are you happy to do three hours a day?"

"Yes, of course."

"Okay then, follow me and I will show you where you can camp."

We followed him on a boardwalk through the jungle. He popped his head in and out of nooks and crannies while looking for an empty place for us to camp until he found a good spot that was available.

"Okay guys, you can camp here. Relax for the day, but come and find me at nine tomorrow morning and I will get you started on your daily chores."

"Thank you," I said, happy to have a place to lay my head.

The property had a tree house at the top of a large old-growth tree. It also had a pyramid, a rope swing, and lots of amazing people. Beside a pond there was a communal kitchen, a telephone with free long distance calls, and a shower. It was outside and had two heads that made each shower feel like you were standing under a waterfall.

The chores were easy – sometimes we would move garbage or wood around or help build and maintain gardens.

I was put in charge of finishing an outhouse that looked like it had been under construction for quite some time.

The commune was a cool place to stay and I enjoyed living there even though we only had a few dollars to our names. We just lived off peanut butter sandwiches, so our food bills stayed small.

Canada Day arrived on the first of July and there was a buzz around the whole town of Tofino. Everybody was planning to party and watch the fireworks but my sister and I weren't even sure if we had enough money left to replenish our supply of bread and peanut butter.

We walked to town to check our bank accounts hoping that we could pool together enough money to at least buy a loaf of bread and a new jar of peanut butter. When I put my card in the machine to check my balance, I was surprised to see that fifty dollars had appeared in my account. It was a miracle! I had received my quarterly tax refund from the Government of Canada's GST rebate. To most, fifty dollars might not seem like much, but at that moment – desperate for just three dollars – we felt as if we had a million bucks. It guaranteed that we could feed ourselves for at least a few weeks.

Since it was Canada Day the subject quickly led to buying some beers to celebrate. My sister and I discussed the possibilities, but in the end we decided that having food for the foreseeable future was more important than getting drunk. We got our supplies and then started the half-hour walk back to the campsite. We had considered going to see the fireworks in town but since we couldn't even afford a drink we decided to just go back to Poole's Land to have a quiet night.

We were halfway home when we passed a man on the sidewalk and said hi. He had a large walking stick and stopped after we wished him a good evening. He had a strange look on his face as he squinted at us in the fading light.

"You know you guys are headed in the wrong direction? The fireworks are that way," he said as he pointed back towards town.

"Yeah we know, but we decided we were just going to have a quiet night."

"Well, enjoy your evening then." But then he paused for a second, reached into his bag, and put a chocolate in my hand. "Maybe this will make your night a little more interesting. It's full of mushrooms," he said with a smile before turning to walk away.

"Wait!" My sister said while looking at me. "Do you want some company?"

"That would be lovely," the man replied in a kind voice.

My sister and I split the chocolate and ate it before we walked back to town with our new friend Joe. We confessed to him that we actually wanted to see the fireworks but had decided against it afraid that we would spend our last few dollars on beer. Joe led us back into town and onto a dock to watch the fireworks with the best possible view.

As soon as we had sat down, Joe offered us more chocolates. Then he pulled out a long glass pipe loaded with bud that he passed our way. I could already feel the chocolate kicking in and I was surprised at how quickly our luck had changed.

The fireworks were great to watch and the reflection of them on the water was a show in itself. I had the thought, "Have you ever seen fireworks, man?" Followed by, "Have you ever seen fireworks on mushrooms, man?" I chuckled to myself.

We spent the whole night out with Joe, then in the early morning we walked back to our tents. When I laid down, I decided that it was time for me to go adventure somewhere else.

I decided to spend one more week in Tofino and I hoped to surf a few more times before we left. We ended up running into Doug on the beach and apologised for leaving abruptly, but he said not to worry about it. He even offered us his boards to use when we wanted to and I realised what a nice guy he truly was.

I had spent almost two months in Tofino and I was happy that I had experienced life by the ocean. I had learned that other types of living arrangements existed than the ones I was used to. A place and way of life where people live comfortably just beyond the fringes of society. A happy life was possible without having a job as long as I was willing to wake up and volunteer for few hours every day. Which I really didn't know if I was. As much fun as it was, I felt like I could just as easily live in the bushes next door with no responsibility and no one to answer to. That was freedom for me, not working for somebody else regardless of how easy the work was. But I was happy I had gone and tried something different. I knew that the more things I tried in life, the more likely it was that I was going to find what I wanted to do in the future. With each day that I tried something new, I felt like I was just a little bit closer to finding out what I wanted to do with the rest of my life.

When I told my sister I was going to go, she had already decided she was going to stay a bit longer with her new love, the ocean. We made a plan to meet a few weeks later before we said goodbye to each other.

I walked back to the highway alone. But it wasn't daunting this time. The road felt more like home than it ever had before. I was happy to go on a little adventure on my own even if it was only just going back to Whistler. In no time at all I was standing on the ferry crossing the Strait of Georgia back to the mainland. By nightfall I had arrived back in Whistler.

THE PEMBERTON FESTIVAL
Pemberton, B.C. 4944 km.

"Pick your life and then fit your job in the cracks. Don't pick your job and then fit your life in the cracks."

My plan was to visit my brother for a few days in Whistler on the way to Shambhala, an annual electronic music festival held at the Salmo River Ranch, a five hundred-acre farm in the West Kootenay mountains. But when I arrived in Whistler with only thirty dollars to my name, I realised that I was going to need some money before I left. Especially since I was getting tired of eating peanut butter sandwiches. I looked in the paper and found an ad for a job at the Pemberton festival in a village just north of Whistler, so I sent in my résumé. A day later I got a phone call.

"Hello," I answered.

"Hi, I'm just calling about a job you applied for at the Pemberton festival."

My heart raced. Say the right thing I thought.

"Which job were you applying for specifically?" the voice asked.

"Oh, umm, which job pays the most?" I replied.

"Oh, that would be more along the lines of store manager."

"Okay, can I apply for that job please?"

I caught the guy off guard. He mumbled a bit and then said "Okay, can you come for an interview at ten tomorrow?"

"Yes, I sure can."

"Great! See you then."

As soon as I got off the phone, I started to prepare for the interview. I went over any questions I thought the guy might ask and got some nice clothes prepared.

The next morning, I woke to bright sunlight shining through the windows. My head was pounding with a horrific hangover and I was on a couch in someone's basement. It took me a while to figure out where I was. Then I remembered that I had a job interview. I had spent the night at my friend Ian's house chugging cans of strong beer and playing foosball. I ran up the stairs to check the time but there was no clock to be found anywhere in the house. I knocked on Ian's door

"Hey man, do you know the time?"

"Uh, it's nine forty," he said.

Shit, I thought, my interview was at ten and my clothes were on the other side of town. Luckily, I was only a block away from where I was supposed to have the appointment.

"Ian," I yelled through his door. "Can I borrow some nice clothes? I've got an interview in fifteen minutes."

Ian's door flew open. He was a lot smaller than I was, but started throwing me any nice clothes he had that he thought I might fit into. Eventually I managed to choose a decent shirt and pants. I walked out the door to the interview where I casually arrived five minutes early.

The interview went well and a day later I got a call from the boss with a start date. Just the thought of getting a pay check and eating some real food again had my mouth watering. Later in the week, my boss Scott picked me up and drove me to the festival site. He was still looking for staff and when I told him that my sister was looking for work as well so he said to bring her over as soon as she could come. I called her and told her to get to Whistler by nightfall if she wanted a job. She said she would try her best.

The inaugural festival site was in the middle of the Pemberton valley, which is surrounded by majestic mountain peaks. It was being held between the twenty-fifth and twenty-seventh of July and there wasn't much time so Scott put everybody to work building and stocking shelves. On the ride he had told me that he hadn't picked who would be in what position yet, and that he would let us know the night before the festival. So when I saw all the workers trying to figure out what to do, I took the reins and started delegating tasks. I put people into teams, some building shelves and others stocking them. I discussed the store plan and ideas with Scott and made sure everything was to his liking and then I jumped in to help.

There was a French guy name Jean that delivered stock to the different stores that were being built. He was a funny dude and we got along from the beginning. He started requesting me as his helper to bring stock around and we would sneak off whenever we could to smoke weed. When Scott announced our positions on the day before the festival, I was named manager at one of the stores and Jean was my assistant manager.

We agreed to camp beside the store we were managing and were responsible for its twenty-four-hour operation. It was well stocked with food, drinks, and cigarettes to keep all the festival goers happy. We set up a couple of camp chairs at the entrance, poured ourselves some drinks, and relaxed.

During the festival Jean and I took turns going to see the bands we wanted to see. The rest of the time we just drank and talked. One day, two of the lovely ladies that worked at my store were moping around looking sad.

"Cheryl, Tammy, are you guys okay? I asked.

"Kind of," they replied, "our lifelong dream is to see Coldplay. In fact, it's the whole reason we came to the festival. We just couldn't afford the tickets. But we asked Scott if we could have the time off and he told us that he needed us to work. So were going to miss the show."

"So? Is that it? You are just not going to go see them?"

"Well, he said we're not allowed!"

"Well, did you come here to work or to see Coldplay?" I asked.

"To see Coldplay," they both said in unison.

"So go see them!"

They looked at me in disbelief and said, "but we're not allowed…?"

I said, "Who cares? Go, follow your dreams! If Scott comes I'll cover for you. If it's really your dream to see them are you seriously just going to take no for an answer?"

"But we're not allowed…" Tammy repeated.

"Well, it doesn't look like I'll need you guys until the shows over, so you're going to have to sign out."

They looked at me, surely wondering what could possibly be going through my head.

"Just go! Don't you want to have some drinks first?" I commanded.

They were hesitant, but when it finally clicked they started jumping up and giggling like schoolgirls before they pranced off.

I watched Tom Petty play later that night. I stood in the crowd with a lighter high in the air singing, "I don't want to live like a refugee." The words reverberated through my body. I felt as if I was alone on the road. The notes of the song were the same as the notes of the road and the road was calling to me again.

I was happy that I had applied for the job at the festival. It allowed me to see countless musicians that I had long dreamed of seeing, made some great new friends, and I had a big pay check on its way, which meant that I could eat something other than peanut butter sandwiches for a little while. It seemed like a great way to go to a festival without the big price tag. I decided that I would do it again somewhere in the future if the opportunity arose.

ANOTHER JOURNEY BEGINS
Whistler, B.C. 4944 km.

"The only goals you don't achieve in life are the goals you don't set."

My sister and I left Whistler the day after we got our paycheques. My brother drove my sister and I to the outskirts of town. I didn't know why I was leaving paradise to go hitchhike again. I had already found what I was looking for, but there was something about the freedom of hitchhiking that I really enjoyed. No schedule, no place to be, and nowhere to go. On the road nothing really matters.

Our plan was to hitchhike to the Shambhala festival not too far from Nelson, B.C., and sneak in. The festival was near a little town called Salmo in the B.C. interior.

We got a ride straight to Pemberton from a guy named Josh and he dropped us off right where the festival had been just days before. The weather was hot and besides the fact that we were getting attacked by black flies the road was as peaceful as life could get. We sat on the side of the road for almost five hours before we finally got a ride. At one point I looked down and noticed my whole package hanging out of a hole in my shorts. It might have been part of the reason that it took so long to get a lift.

From there we hit the jackpot. A girl named Holly picked us up and was going seven hundred km in the direction we wanted to go. It was perfect. The evergreen trees disappeared and were replaced by a red rocky canyon that was dangerously steep. The road seemed as if it was barely carved into the edge of the canyon and the massive Fraser River raged below us.

My sister Nicole sat in the front with Holly while I slept in the back, only periodically joining in on the conversation when I was awake. When Holly arrived at the turn off to Kelowna she dropped us off on the side of the highway.

There was no good place to camp. It was night time and neither of us felt like jumping a barb wire fence in the dark. Without doing so the easiest spot to camp was beside the three-foot tall cement barrier on the edge of the highway. It was a horrible idea. We spent the night listening to cars speeding past dangerously close to us while the ground rumbled beneath. It was not a pleasant place to sleep. At the break of dawn, we packed up our tent and decided that we would never camp so close to a road again.

The next morning, we walked down the on ramp, the same ramp that I walked up almost a year before. Lake Okanagan was as beautiful as ever and stretched as far as the eye could see. After a short while I got a ride from a farmer named Ben.

"You know I've got a tree that grows four different types of fruit!" he told us while driving.

"Really?"

"Yup, I can graft a branch from one tree onto another, all farmers know how to do it."

We took his word for it and a little while later he dropped us off in Penticton. I realised we were only fifteen km away from Naramata – the little town where the French girls from Tofino were fruit picking. It felt great to have no timeline and nothing to worry about. I felt way more comfortable hitchhiking than I had the year before and I was a little more confident that things would work out for the best. We were welcomed to Naramata by the smell of blossoming fruit trees. The trip had been easy and my sister was more excited about hitchhiking than ever before.

LOVE UNDER THE STARS
Naramata B.C. 5473 km.

"Confidence is simply just believing in yourself."

Naramata is a small farming town with a single store and a fruit warehouse. We got a hold of Jennifer on the pay phone late in the day and she gave us directions to her place, which was a few blocks from town.

Jennifer and her sister were working as cleaners instead of fruit picking as they had planned, partly because they got paid more and partly because they were offered a free place to stay as a perk of the job. Sadly for me they weren't allowed to have guests. So when we met up she led us to a secluded beach on the shores of Lake Okanagan and assured us that we could camp there for a few nights without any trouble.

We walked onto the beach just as the sun was setting. I pulled out a bottle of wine, opened it up, and we passed it back and forth. Jennifer gave me the sexy eyes and I knew it was on. We all shared two bottles of wine and spent the night giggling and laughing in the warm weather under the stars.

Eventually Jennifer and I went for a walk along the beach where we found a private little cove and we kissed. Then we laid down beside each other and caressed each other's smooth skin. Piece by piece we took off each other's clothing until we were both naked in the moonlight. My whole body tingled as we made passionate love beside the water's edge. It was like a scene out of a movie.

After some cuddles we put our clothes back on and joined our respective sisters where we had left them. Jennifer had to work early so we made plans for the next day before they left. Then my sister and I finished off the wine and went to sleep on the beach.

I woke up to a colourful sunrise and a panoramic view of the glassy lake with the rolling hills in the distance. It was the most beautiful place I had ever woken up to, our own isolated beach in paradise. I grabbed a drink out of my water bottle and put my head back down on my sand pillow. There was no rush to wake up, I was comfy, and the air temperature was perfect.

We spent a few more days in Naramata. My sister and I enjoyed our time swimming in the lake and bathing in the sun. In the evening I would sneak off to meet Jennifer for our nightly sexual escapades somewhere out in nature. Wherever we could find a semi-private place to get naked, we got naked. Life was pretty good.

MANIFESTING SHAMBHALA
Naramata, B.C. 5473 km.

"Follow your intuition, it will always take you where you need to go."

On the day we were leaving town, Jennifer dropped us off on the side of the highway at six in the morning. She didn't say one word the whole trip and I could tell by the look on her face that she was sad to see me go. I was going to miss her too. We hugged and said our goodbyes before the girls drove off forever.

As soon as we got out onto the side of the highway, I noticed the strong smell of smoke and I could feel my eyes burning. I looked around and noticed the whole valley was smoky. It looked as though there was a large forest fire burning nearby. We waited on the side of the road in the smoke, but by lunch no car had pulled over. We found an old-fashioned hamburger joint up the street and got a burger and fries. Eating something other than peanut butter sandwiches made me feel like a king.

When we had finished eating and were back on the road waiting, a girl named Wendy picked us up in an old station wagon. It must have been from the eighties, but it had some guts under the hood. Wendy wasn't going far, but she assured us that she could take us to a better hitchhiking spot than the one that we were in.

She dropped us off in the wilderness surrounded by forest. Before she drove off, she said, "I'm sending you good vibes so you get the perfect ride." One ride was better than none and I was already happy that we had made any distance. The sun was getting lower in the sky and it was starting to look like we were going to be spending the night where we were.

I noticed a neat rock formation on the other side of the road so I went to explore it. I climbed up the steep embankment through sandy, dry soil until I arrived at the top of a cliff. I posed like I had just hiked Mount Everest to make my sister laugh. But as I was posing, all the sand underneath my feet gave away and I started to slide towards the edge. A second before I was about to slip over I jumped, hoping to direct my landing somewhere safe and hopefully in between the rocks scattered below.

The impact was hard, the drop looked to be twice my height, yet I miraculously avoided injuring myself. I decided to go and continue to wait with my sister, it seemed a little safer back on the other side of the road. Just as I started crossing a purple Hyundai stopped. The guy looked at me and said through his open window, "That was sweet dude, where are you guys headed?"

"Shambhala," I replied.

"Well hop in, that's where I'm going."

The good vibes Wendy had sent us must have worked.

The guy driving was named Jono, and as soon as we got in the car he started to tell us a story. "Last year, one of my friends was heading to the festival with a car full of drugs. But he took a wrong turn and ended up crossing the border into the United States. Everyone in the car was freaking out, but the border was closed so they ended up getting back across without anybody noticing. So just a heads up in case you notice I'm going across the border, just let me know!"

I wondered how we were going to get into the festival. I had heard that security was almost impossible to get past and we had no knowledge of what the place looked like. The pitch-black night didn't help either. But maybe the dark could be our ticket in.

SNEAKING INTO SHAMBHALA
Salmo, B.C. 5807 km.

"The toughest challenges bring the greatest rewards."

As we got closer, we started to see signs directing us towards the festival entrance. Eventually we arrived at what looked like a private driveway. We followed the dark gravel road for five kilometres, at which point Jono pulled the car over. "All right guys, this is probably the best spot for you to get out. Those lights up ahead are the main gate so there will be a lot of security nearby. When there are no cars around us, jump out. Hide in the dark, and don't use lights as they will give you away. Good luck!"

When the last car drove by, we jumped out and ran into the forest. We watched Jono drive away, then we sat in the bushes and waited while we let our eyes adjust to the darkness. As we sat there, I wondered how I came up with such crazy ideas. Surely there had to be an easier way to get in? But my friend had told me that it was impossible to sneak in, so I had accepted the challenge. For that reason alone, we were at the gates of Shambhala.

We crossed the gravel road, then jumped the wooden fence. I was engulfed by the smell of fresh horse dung. We crept slowly and quietly through the paddock until we reached a forest on the other side. Then we stopped and crouched in the bushes while we assessed our surroundings just as a car's headlights lit up the whole field we had just walked through.

In an attempt to become invisible, we trekked deeper into the forest. We could see the main gate of the festival through the trees, lit up with spotlights. We walked quietly through the forest until we arrived at another clearing. It was pitch black and totally exposed to the line-up of cars waiting at the gates. We walked through the clearing as quietly as possible until we arrived at a massive hole in the ground that was directly in our path. It looked like a good place to get some cover, so we crept into it. It turned out to be full of baseball-sized rocks. The odd rock slipped a little but we made it to the bottom in almost total silence.

The only problem was that getting out of the hole as quietly as we got in was impossible. We took the first few steps, but the rocks tumbled down loudly and we froze. After a quick chat about what to do, we ran up the side at full speed. Rocks crashed and tumbled with every step. It seemed as though I was sliding down half a step for every step forward I took. A lot of the rocks tumbled back into the middle of the pit, crashing and banging in the silent night.

When we finally made it to the top, we sprinted towards the forest just as two security pick-up trucks came racing into the field. "Get down," I yelled to my sister. We dove into the long grass with our bags still on our backs. The trucks turned on their spotlights and the grass around us lit up like it was daytime. I was sure that we were busted. The truck's engines went silent and I heard their doors open and shut, then there was silence. I whispered to my sister, "Don't move."

A torturous ten minutes passed in total silence. It sounded like the security guards had vanished while we waited patiently. Then I heard rocks tumbling down the gravel pit – the first sign that they were still around. This was followed by more footsteps, slowly moving closer to us. I saw flashlights beams swing crazily all around us. My heart raced and I waited for a hand to grab my shoulder. But it didn't happen, the flashlights went elsewhere and then everything became silent. We heard a few doors shut, then the trucks engines started and the sound of gravel crunching under the trucks tires as they drove off. Once again, we were left in the silent and dark night.

After a minute or two I whispered to my sister, "Don't move." We waited another ten minutes in total silence. Then all of a sudden we heard another set of footsteps walking away from us. They must have been pretty close, so we waited a bit longer just to be sure. Then when we were sure that the coast was clear we grabbed our stuff and jumped over a fallen tree at the edge of the forest.

We landed quietly and then sat still, waiting and

listening. My eyes had adjusted to the darkness and I could see more than I could before. We heard a few more rocks clattering in the gravel pit, either security was still looking for us or another person was following the same route we did.

When we were sure the coast was clear we crept silently into the forest. I couldn't believe security had been so close but didn't see us lying in the grass with our massive backpacks sticking out.

We trekked deeper into the woods until we arrived at a big culvert. I could make out shadows of people walking past, but wasn't sure if they were people sneaking in or security still lurking around. We made a dash to the other side of the culvert and walked straight into the dense forest. We continued over logs, under branches, through bushes, and we squeezed through the dense undergrowth.

I had no idea where we were, my only guide was the pulse of the bass in the distance. We walked for some time and the foliage got even thicker.

"I'm exhausted and my knee hurts," my sister told me.

We had started at six that morning and it had been a very long day.

"If we keep going, we could be in within the hour," I reassured her.

"Nah, I'm too tired. Can we set up camp for the night and continue in the morning?"

I knew that the cover of darkness provided us with the best opportunity to sneak in. But my sister insisted and as much as I wanted to go and dance, I wasn't going to leave her alone in a forest at night.

Since we didn't want to give away our position in the forest by setting up our tents, we decided to sleep under the tarp. The ground was covered in soft moss and pine needles that seemed like a perfect mattress. Just as we put the tarp over us to sleep, we heard the crack of thunder, lightning lit up the sky, and torrential rain poured down. Amazingly, the tarp kept us completely dry.

My sister had made a great decision. If we had still been walking through the woods as I had hoped, we would have been drenched, cold, and exhausted. I fell asleep to rain drops pattering the tarp and woke up to the sun shining through the trees in the morning. There was nobody around us when we got up so we packed up the tarp and tried to figure out which way to go.

Since we were in the middle of the forest, every direction looked pretty much the same. So like the night before in the dark we just followed the music. After a while we made it out of the forest into a clearing. We could see the main entrance to the festival just beyond some trees to our right. There were cars lined up at the security checkpoint and guards were everywhere. The guards were all focused on the cars at the gate so we ran full speed through the clearing past a barn then we descended into a thick patch of bushes, moving as fast as we could. We arrived at a stream next to an embankment. Just above us there was a road full of people that had already passed through the main checkpoint.

I ran up onto the road when a group was passing and asked, "Hey man, are we in yet?"

"Not yet," came the reply, "you still have to go through that checkpoint up there," he said as he pointed to another gate with a security guard sitting at it. "Thanks," I muttered. I jumped back down the embankment.

We spent the rest of the day trekking through bushes, forests, and swamps trying to find a way in. The day was a scorcher, we were boiling hot, drenched in filthy swamp water, and we stank. On top of that we realised that after a day of trudging through the woods we were trapped on the wrong side of a deep swamp. We had already been battling the bushes for over sixteen hours and we felt like we had lost. We decided to head back to the spot by the embankment and two hours later we found it again. We were hungry, thirsty, and tired, but happy we weren't lost in the woods anymore.

Just like earlier in the day I jumped up onto the road. "Are we in yet?" I asked a stranger.

"Yup," the guy said. "What? Really?" I replied. He repeated the same answer, "Yup." I was in disbelief. I ran back down to my sister and said, "Let's just try it." We waited for the perfect moment, and when a group of people were walking past we ran up onto the road and joined them.

My heart was racing as we approached the security guard. The only way in, and the last barrier that blocked us. We got closer, the music got louder, my heart raced faster. "Walk past him like you own the place," I said to my sister.

We walked in. The security guard didn't even look at us. We had arrived in a valley of tents surrounded by hills covered in evergreen trees. Without any hesitation, we disappeared into the field of tents. When we found a good spot to camp, we dropped our bags, exhausted.

The taste of success was sweet. It almost made not buying tickets seem worthwhile. Without the struggle I wondered if I would have felt as good as I did at that moment. I realised that the harder the challenge, the more I enjoyed the success. Perhaps that was why I kept hitchhiking. It was a life where success was the prize in return for persistence, determination, and patience.

A fairy walked by followed by a cheetah and then a unicorn. Where had we arrived? I wondered. Many people were dressed up in costumes and most of them said hi when we crossed paths.

After setting up our tents and resting for a while, we went to wander the festival. We found a stage along the river that had electronic music playing. There were people swimming in the water, dancing in front of the stage, and spinning fire. I noticed a guy with big dreads sitting beside the stage with a massive bag of weed that he was selling to a line of people. Nothing seemed real in Shambhala. I got in line and waited my turn.

There were five stages that each played music for twenty-three hours a day. Bassnectar was playing at one stage and after we found it, we made our way up to the front. The place was wild, the bass drops were out of this world, and the crowd seemed to be tapped into some eternal energy source. I danced like I had never danced before along with the people around me. It felt as if I was developing a deep connection with them as we danced.

I danced at all the different stages, constantly moving to find the music I preferred the most. My level of intoxication escalated as the kind souls I danced with offered what they had. At some point in the night I became lost at a stage called the Labyrinth and I quickly understood why it had its name. I walked in circles, but there didn't seem to be a way out. In the light of the day it was like any other stage, but in the darkness it was all that existed. After a while I realised that I kept passing the same guy. Was he trying to get out of the Labyrinth as well? I wondered. I decided to ask the next time our paths crossed. It didn't take long.

"Hey man!"

"Hey, how are you?"

"Good thanks, I just noticed we keep walking past each other," I said. "Are you trying to get out of here as well?" His eyes looked like they had been shattered by copious amounts of drugs.

"Yeah man, I've been going in circles for ever. I just want some water!"

"Me too! Do you want to join forces? I'm desperate for a drink too."

We walked off together. With two inebriated minds we had the brain power of almost a whole person. It didn't take long for us to escape and soon after we got some water. We spent the rest of the night wandering the festival together, dancing the night away until the sun came up.

I crawled into my tent long after the sun had risen. It must have been close to noon and I was exhausted. The tent was too hot to be in, so I slept with half my body inside and half out. At some point it started to rain, but I didn't move. The rain cooled and refreshed me and I spent half the day drifting in and out of sleep while listening to the music in the distance.

While I laid there, I remembered that less than a day before I had been lost in the woods, drenched, boiling, filthy, and tired. But all that had changed. I slept for a good part of the day and just as the sun was getting lower in the sky, I dragged myself out of the tent and headed back towards the music.

There was a fire show at the river stage, people were spinning fireballs, staffs, swords, and whips. One guy spun eight fireballs at the same time perfectly. It was insane to watch. I saw a girl I knew from Whistler named Heidi who had long blonde dreads and we ended up hanging out for a good part of the night.

Shambhala was a life-changing experience. There was so much love at the festival it was almost overwhelming. Everybody I met had been so welcoming and friendly. It was like no place I had ever been before. Everybody seemed to care so much about everybody else, and I dreamed of a world where everybody did the same. When the festival was over, I felt like a whole new person – calm, relaxed, and more in tune with my intuition.

My sister and I packed up our bags slowly in the hot late summer sun. We weren't in a rush to go anywhere since we didn't have anywhere to be. We wandered to the gates of the festival and got a ride to the only gas station in town where we joined a bunch of hitchhikers already waiting on the road. We decided to go to Nelson about fifty km to the north to check the town out and eventually a camper van pulled over that was going straight there. They filled it with as many people as they could possibly fit including my sister and myself. Then the old camper slowly started to move.

THEN THERE WERE THREE
Nelson, B.C. 5848 km.

"Take a chance with someone, you never know where it may lead."

Heidi, the girl I knew from Whistler, had ended up in the camper with us. When we got dropped off in Nelson we all decided to hang out together. After searching, we found a place to camp on a private beach on the edge of an old industrial property. It seemed like a safe place to leave our stuff. Climbing up and down a decrepit metal structure was the only way to gain access to the shoreline. I didn't imagine that too many people would go through the effort to steal our meagre possessions.

We set up our tents in the sand only a few feet away from the edge of the water and I hoped that the level of the lake didn't rise for any reason. Then we sat in the sun and enjoyed our beachfront accommodation. After a quick audit I realised that I had spent most of the money I had earned at the Pemberton festival. I needed to start budgeting again if

I wanted to keep eating.

We spent a few days in Nelson by the lake recovering from the festival, while my sister and I contemplated different routes to follow on the map. She suggested going to Alaska. I was tempted, but I knew she had to catch a flight from Calgary in a few weeks and the distance seemed almost impossible to travel in such a short amount of time.

Heidi didn't know what she was going to do after Nelson either.

"Do you want to come hitchhiking with us?" I asked

"Hmm, maybe – where are you going next?" Heidi asked.

"We just have to be in Calgary for my sister's flight, other than that I'm down for anything.

We discussed the idea with my sister and when we all decided that it could be fun, we planned to hit the road. I didn't actually know if hitchhiking with three people was possible, but there was only one way to find out.

LIGHT THEM BOTH UP
Slocan, B.C. 5917 km.

"If you make time for everybody, more people will make time for you."

We walked to the outskirts of Nelson and began a long wait by the side of the road, all the while wondering if we were actually going to get a ride with all three of us. Our question was answered when we got picked up by a girl named Melissa who had also just been to Shambhala. She took us to a little town called Crescent Valley about fifteen km from Nelson and then pulled into a gravel car park beside a river.

"Do you guys want to come for a swim?" she asked. "We have a bunch of inflated inner tubes down by the river you're welcome to use if you like."

I looked at the girls and they both smiled. "Yeah, that would be amazing – thanks!"

We grabbed our bags and followed Melissa down to the river. When we arrived at the water's edge, Melissa's friends were having a picnic and they offered us the inner tubes. We floated down the river on the tubes for about an hour and when we were content, we walked back up to the road. There was a fruit stand right in front of us so we took advantage of it. I walked away with some ripe peaches then sat on the side of the road, more interested in eating the fruit than getting a ride.

A middle-aged guy named Jeff pulled over in an old school red pick-up truck. He was wearing a straw hat, a red plaid shirt, he had tanned skin, and he looked like a farmer.

"Where are you headed?" I asked, leaning into the window. "Just the next town over, but I'm happy to take you as far as I go," Jeff replied with friendly smile. "You can squeeze in here with me if you like," he said referring to the bench seat upfront. It was the only seat that the truck had. We put our bags in the back and squeezed together on the bench seat.

We had only driven a few kilometres when Jeff said, "You guys want to take the back roads and have a puff along the way?"

"Sounds good to us," we replied, smiling.

He pulled the truck over. "Can you roll?" he asked

"Yup," I replied.

"All right, roll two then," he said as he threw a small bag on my lap. When I was done rolling, he started the truck and we drove off.

"Light them both up," Jeff said. The joints went around and around. As soon as I passed one on, the other arrived – I could barely keep up with them. Eventually we were all super stoned. "Now this is how to go on a road trip!" Jeff said enthusiastically, clearly excited to be a part of our adventure. We continued north until we reached Slocan B.C. where Jeff dropped us off on the side of the highway before he went into the town.

Our day had been a great success, so instead of hitching any more we decided to go hang out for the afternoon and find a place to camp for the night. We walked the same road that Jeff had driven down into the village of Slocan, B.C. There was one little shop where we got a bunch of discounted food that had nearly expired.

After some exploring, we found a big lake that fed a small river. It was the most beautiful spot we had found up to that point, so we decided to set up camp there. I made some peanut butter sandwiches and we ate dinner while the sun set over the mountains. When dusk arrived, we set up our tents and fell asleep to the sound of the burbling river.

We spent the next morning floating in the clear blue water. Nearby there was an old guy painting so I said, "hi."

"Good morning," he said with a smile before getting down to business.

"You know you're right in the middle of an alien hotspot here?" he said with a serious look on his face.

"No, I didn't know that. What do you mean?" I replied kindly.

"Well, over the years aliens have frequented the area. I've seen them – all shapes and sizes. The government tries to cover it up, but I've seen them with my own two eyes." I wondered if maybe he had, anything was possible.

When we were all ready to go, we made our way back to

the highway. Almost straight away we got a ride in a red convertible sports car from a businesswoman named Anna. She was driving home from a conference she had been to in Vancouver. It was nice to watch the mountains go by with the wind blowing in my hair while sitting on the comfy leather seats. Ah, the luxuries of hitchhiking, I thought. Anna drove us to a town called Nakusp, B.C. which was on the shore of Arrow Lake and when we got there she asked, "Do you want to stay on the highway or come into town?"

"The highway please," we answered, hoping to cover a bit more distance.

We waited for hours, but all the cars that went by seemed to turn off the highway and head into the little town. We searched up the road for a better spot to hitch, but it got narrow and the shoulders disappeared. We decided to go back to our initial spot where we just sat and waited some more. Sometime later a red Chrysler Neon pulled over. A guy stuck his head out of the window and said, "I don't have much time, but I can take you to a better hitchhiking spot if you like, you're never going to get a ride here." We gladly accepted the lift and got in the car.

"You guys are on the wrong side of town," the guy named Les explained once we were moving. "Everybody goes straight through town and out the other side, people always get stuck hitching at that spot. I'm just on my way to work or I would take you further."

"Thanks, we appreciate it. Where do you work?" I asked.

"I trim buds."

"Nice man! Any extra jobs?" I asked thinking of the small

amount of money left in my bag.

"Oh, sorry man, you've got to know the guy."

Ah, well I thought, it was worth a try.

When we got to the other side of town, Les said. "Actually, now that I think about it there is a campground up the road, it's free and right on the lake. I can take you there if you like."

"Cool man, that would be awesome!" I said after making sure the girls liked the idea.

He drove a bit further up the road that was lined with evergreen trees and dropped us off at the entrance to the campground. We walked down the driveway towards the shore where we were blessed with panoramic views of Arrow Lake, its turquoise water surrounded by towering, majestic mountains peaks. The view was magnificent.

Once our tents were set up, we made a bonfire at the water's edge, then drank a few beers under the stars. The next morning, I woke up to the sound of the girls playing in the water. I stuck my head out of the tent and was welcomed by a warm sunny day. I sat on the shore to take in the view while I listened to the sounds of nature around me. The birds chirped, frogs sang, and fish jumped. I was in a place that I would be happy to never leave. I knew all that I needed to be happy was a tent, some food, a few friends, and nature. I had a clear mind, I was content, and I was happy. A year before I would not have felt the same in such a remote part of the world with a long and empty road ahead of me.

After playing in the water for a good part of the day, we packed our bags and hit the highway. I noticed a crystal-clear stream beside the road and I filled up our water bottles. I didn't know if it was a good idea or not, but I was thirsty and I knew I would find out in a day or two if it was a mistake.

A blue pick-up pulled over and when I walked up to the window I realised it was already full of people.

"Hi, looks pretty full," I said.

"The trucks full, but you're welcome to sit in the back, I'm going a fair way up the road," the driver said.

It was a tempting offer considering how few cars had passed by. We figured since he had his kids in the back, he would probably be driving safe so we accepted his offer.

We jumped in the back with our bags and the truck drove off. I could see the mountains over the tree tops and the view was spectacular the whole trip. It was one of the best rides I ever had.

Eventually the truck stopped and dropped us off. Just as we sat down on the road a small red car pulled over. There were two girls in it named Stef and Tiff and they had also just been to Shambhala.

"Get in quickly, were trying to make it to the ferry on time," Tiff said.

They were headed to Golden, B.C. and happy to drive us to Revelstoke on the way. I was surprised that we had been getting rides so easily with three of us. I thought that it was going to be a lot harder. But perhaps having two girls on the side of the road actually makes hitchhiking easier. Maybe I seem less scary with two girls beside me.

We pulled up to a line of cars and waited for the ferry.

Once we boarded, the view was magical – the rays of the late afternoon sun reflected off the glassy-smooth water, while the loud engines churned beneath us. Through my eyes I saw total calm and peaceful bliss and through my ears I heard the loud creation of man roaring beneath me, taking us to the other side.

KERRY AND PREACHER
Revelstoke, B.C. 6100 km.

"If you can find beauty in everything, everything will seem more beautiful to you."

We arrived in Revelstoke, about a hundred km from Nakusp, just as the sun set. The girls dropped us off near downtown. It was a small place with a few blocks of shops in the town centre. We went to get some beers for the evening and just as we left the store a man pushing a shopping cart said, "Hi."

"Hi," I answered back.

"Hey, do you guys want some liquor? Or some beer? Or maybe some food?" I didn't know how to respond to a seemingly homeless person offering us something to eat. The shopping cart was full of the guy's belongings and his dog walked by his side. When he noticed the look of bewilderment on our faces, he said, "Read the sign." He pointed to a piece of cardboard attached to his cart. It said that he was walking across Canada to bring more awareness to the problem of homelessness.

"By the way, my names Kerry and this is my dog Preacher. Are you sure you don't want some food or a drink?"

"Nah, thanks though, we have money and food, were just hitching for the adventure."

"What about an extra blanket? A tent? Socks? I've got it all," he said smiling.

"Nah, thanks again man, we have all that we need. Well, we've got to get going so have a good night." He seemed like a nice guy, but it had been a long day and I didn't really feel like talking to anybody. I just wanted to go find a place to camp.

We wandered off in search of a place to pitch our tent. At the edge of town, we found a private property with a little forest in the front, so we decided to camp there. We set up our tents, grabbed our drinks, then walked back to town.

We planned to pre-drink somewhere and then go to check out one of the bars in town. But when we got back into town we came across Kerry again.

"Hey guys, what are you up too?" he said as he came rushing over to us. My first thought was to avoid him because I didn't feel like being social but he arrived before we could get away.

"I'm having a drink on the sidewalk over there, you're welcome to join me," he said. I looked at the girls and they shrugged, so we joined him.

We sat down on the sidewalk with Kerry. He offered us some whiskey, but we turned it down and pulled out our own booze.

"You're walking across Canada to raise awareness about homelessness?" I asked.

"Yep, pretty much. I'm a carpenter by trade. Spent most of my life working hard to provide for my family. Then one day I realised that I'd spent all my time working and that I didn't really know my family anymore and they didn't really know me. We had grown apart, even though I worked hard for them every day. Things weren't going well with my wife so I just left. Times got hard and I ended up on the streets for a while. Now I'm trying to bring awareness to the struggle other people like me have."

"The road gets lonely sometimes though," he continued, "that's why I made an effort to talk to you guys – you looked nice and to be honest I don't see that many people on the road. I just talk to my dog for the most part."

The drinks flowed and we played music while we talked about life. We ended up spending the whole evening with Kerry. Every once and a while a police cruiser would drive past slowly and stare at us. I thought they were going to come and say something because we were drunk and singing at the top of our lungs but they didn't.

"Where are you going to sleep tonight?" I asked Kerry.

"Right where I'm sitting, I don't even have to move. I'm already on my blanket."

"Why don't you go camp in the woods, somewhere beautiful?" I asked.

"There is no more beauty in the woods than there is in the concrete that I'm sitting on," Kerry replied.

"Really?" I asked, confused by his statement.

"There is beauty in everything, you just have to look for it. For example, the reason we are looking at those woods is because we travelled over concrete and pavement to get here. It's the concrete in warehouses that shelters the space we use to produce and store the food we eat. We go to concrete buildings to buy our food. Our waste and sewage goes down concrete pipes. We also live in those concrete buildings. Without concrete our society would stop, it keeps it going. Just like the tree that gives us oxygen, the concrete is a necessity as well. I see what it does for us as a species and in a sense, it is beautiful."

"That makes sense I guess, but it might take me a little while to digest the concept."

I thought of how I perceived the world. Could I also find beauty in anything? I was sad to say I couldn't. I wondered how he could possibly see so much beauty in something that destroyed nature. Maybe Kerry knew something I didn't. Was it because of his experiences?

Kerry had been playing my sister's drum for most of the night and we could tell he loved it. "I have never played a drum before, it's quite a magical experience," he said while enthusiastically drumming away on it. "I might buy one the next chance I get," he told us.

When our drinks were done and we were ready to go to bed, we thanked Kerry for the great company and the wise words that he provided. Right before we walked away, my sister gave Kerry her drum and said, "This was meant for you."

He said, "Thank you, it means more than you will ever know." We walked away with smiles on our faces, then climbed back up the hill to our tents.

FALLING DOWN
Banff, Alberta. 6383 km.

"The best intentions don't always lead to the best outcomes."

There was no good place to hitchhike out of town, just a highway with no shoulder. After we tried a few different spots, we decided to wait beside the stop lights, hoping to get a ride from someone waiting for them to turn green. Eventually our plan worked and we got a ride in a minivan that was going straight to Banff.

After we got dropped off, we stashed our bags in some bushes, grabbed our swimming gear, and wandered into town. We planned on sneaking into a hot tub at the Fairmont Banff Springs, which was the nicest and grandest hotel in town. So we got a bottle of wine, a few beers, and walked towards the hotel.

There was only a fence separating the Fairmont's hot tub from the forest. So we found a path that led into the bushes behind the hotel and followed it. The path was less than a foot wide with a steep drop to a raging river below. We carefully shimmied along it in the dark while we listened to the noise of the river. We had almost arrived at the hot tub when I heard my sister scream. She went over the edge and I could hear her shrieks as she tumbled down the near vertical slope.

I spun and blindly jumped over the edge into the darkness while aiming in the direction of my sister's screams. While I flew through the air I wondered if jumping off the edge was a good idea. But I didn't know how far the river was below and if my sister went in, I wanted to be there beside her. I hit the ground hard, then crashed into some trees. I managed to wrap my arm around one of them to slow down. I could hear my sister still screaming and tumbling down the hill. I jumped again, yelling, "Nicole!" while I flew through the air. I crashed again, stopped, and waited for a response.

"Over here," I heard her mumble. I ran up to her side and asked, "Are you okay?"

"Kind of," she said. She was shaken up, but luckily managed to avoid any serious injury. I helped her get to her feet and we climbed back up to the path together. I was happy that she was okay. But once we got back to the sidewalk she stormed off. "I've had enough of your crazy ideas!" she told me as she took off down the street. Heidi and I gave chase and tried to console her.

I didn't know what to do – I was supposed to look out for her best interests. A year earlier she had become so intrigued by my hitchhiking adventures she had decided that she was going to do it too. It worried me. I knew the road was dangerous. I had met a few female hitchhikers and they all had scary stories of predatory creeps and weirdos. So after discussing it with her, I had agreed to take her hitchhiking with me to give her the experience, knowing that I would look out for her safety. I felt like I had failed in that task. When I caught up with Nicole she said, "Look, I'm not that upset about the fall or even your crazy ideas, I just lost a gem stone that I had when I fell and it meant a lot to me."

"That's okay, I'll go look for it."

I went back into the bushes, alone this time but with a flashlight. I walked down the same path and climbed down the steep slope. I scoured the ground until I saw her stone. The odds of finding it were astronomical so I brought it back to her with a smile and then we walked back to our bags in silence.

I was stressed from the events of the night and I was happy when I finally got into bed. I hoped that the next day would be better. We were about one hundred km from Calgary and we still had a few days before we had to be there for my sister's flight. The day before she had told me that she had enjoyed hitchhiking so much that she planned to do more after our trip. It was the last thing I wanted to hear. I had hoped that our journey together would have satisfied her curiosity and that she would choose a normal life once it was out of her system rather than the road. But I was not there to make her decisions for her, I just hoped that she would never have to experience the dangerous side of hitchhiking.

FEAR
Banff, Alberta. 6383 km.

"There are lessons within everything if you take the time to find them."

The next morning, I crawled out of my tent onto freshly cut wet grass. It looked like it was going to be a nice day. After we packed up our tents, we ate breakfast beside the river and then decided to go for a swim.

We all climbed into the icy glacier-fed river. The temperature was a shock, but the water was refreshing. I fought the urge to get out at least until I had washed myself. We had only been in the water for a minute when a guy looked down on us from the riverbank and said, "Hey guys, can I come swim too?" He was pale with yellow decaying teeth, skinny and was dressed in a black shirt with black pants. I thought it was a strange question considering the size of the river and the fact that it's a free world. He didn't need to ask us permission, he was welcome to do whatever he wanted.

"Sure," I responded, just to be polite. He took his pants off down to his boxers and jumped in the water just as the girls and I got out. A moment later, the stranger got out of the water as well.

The girls and I changed quickly then packed our bags for our journey.

"You guys want to head to the highway?" I asked the girls.

"Yep, let's do it," they replied.

The strange guy was nearby, still in his wet boxers. When I looked at him, I noticed that he had half an erection. It was disturbing. I told the girls and they were appalled. We grabbed our stuff and started walking towards the highway.

We crossed the street and walked down the on ramp. It was a long ramp, with lots of room for cars to pull over. We worked out the best place to stand, then dropped our bags and put our thumbs out. I was glad we were leaving Banff. The night before had been stressful and I was looking forward to arriving somewhere with better vibes than the ones we were leaving behind.

We had only been on the highway for a few minutes when the guy from the river rode up to us on his bike. He put his bike down on the edge of the highway and then walked towards us. I thought it was strange that he had followed us and I was trying to figure out why he did that.

When he got close, he started circling us without saying a word. Then without warning he said, "Go hitchhike further down the highway," in a menacing voice.

"Actually," I said, "we're in the best spot to get a ride

right here, so I think it's better if we just stay."

Then he started telling us random facts about his life.

"You know, I used to live on an island off the coast of Vancouver," he said and then paused. "Bad things happened there, real bad things," he mumbled.

We watched him in silence.

"You don't know where I've been! You don't know what I've done!" he said with a newfound intensity. "I've killed someone you know! That bastard shouldn't have messed with me! The islands have their own laws!"

I watched him intensely, following every step he took. He was clearly a madman. He continued to circle us while speaking nonsense. I watched him as he pulled a little rope out of his pocket. It was about half an inch thick and it had a loop at each end. He put a few fingers through each end of it. Then he continued circling us. I stared at the rope. I was sure I had seen something like it before. In a movie perhaps. I racked my brain.

Why did he just tell us that he had killed someone? Why did he follow us to the highway? Why did he have an erection at the river? I didn't like the vibe I was getting from him one bit or the tone of voice he was using. I felt like we were in imminent danger.

He continued with his crazy talk, "one night this guy messed with me, he made a bad decision, he shouldn't have fucked with me." A shiver went up my spine. "I killed him!" he said with anger and certainty.

I looked into his eyes and could tell he was insane. He looked crazier than before, like he had smoked a ton of crack or meth or something. Then he repeated the words he had said before, but louder, "I just fuckin' told you, you should go and hitchhike further down the highway." This time he pointed in the direction he wanted us to go.

He began walking faster while he circled us still staring at us with his crazy eyes. I wondered why he was circling us. Why he had the rope in his hand? Why he had just told us he killed someone again? I knew his presence was threatening. I knew something was wrong. Protect the girls at all costs, I thought to myself. It felt as if he was waiting for the right moment to pounce. Then all of a sudden it clicked. The rope was to strangle someone.

I told the girls my thoughts and they agreed with me. I asked Heidi for her knife, but it was only a small Swiss Army knife and I figured it was best kept hidden. I thought of the big machete I carried when I first went hitchhiking, but I had left it behind. I clenched my fists, ready to attack him the second he made the wrong move. Then he walked off the highway and into the long grass.

"Girls, I think he's a total psycho with bad intentions. If he makes one wrong move I'm going to attack him and take him to the ground. At that moment, you both run onto the highway and stop traffic. Find a trustworthy lady driver to take you to safety and call the cops. Please, just get away while you have the chance. Don't worry about me, I can handle myself."

At that point he came out of the grass with two rocks. He then smashed them on the road a few times until he ended up with two softball-sized chunks that fit perfectly into his hands. He continued walking circles around us again, this time while clacking the rocks together menacingly. He had an even crazier look in his eye than before.

I clenched my jaw and furrowed my brow with anger. Then I stared deep into his eyes with a menacing glare. He was really starting to piss me off. I wanted him to know that he was not going to win. I wanted him to understand that I was no longer calm and smiling and that we were not going to be his prey. With every step he took I spun around, following him. Danger was imminent and all I knew was that it was going to be him or it was going to be me.

Then he almost yelled, "For the last time, would you go hitchhike down there!" It seemed like a trap. Why down there? I wanted to be in the spot that I chose, not his. But he said it like it was our last chance. I was not going to leave the warning unheeded if violence could be avoided.

I responded with a raised voice, "Okay, we'll go over there! But only if you stay here! We'll never get a ride with four people!" I tried to deflect attention away from the situation with my words while trying to confuse his demented mind.

"Grab your bags girls, let's go!" We backed slowly away until at least fifteen feet separated us. Then we jogged until we were at the end of the on ramp, where we stopped.

"Girls," I said, "I know we're in a scary situation and that guy is clearly insane. I am super shaken up too. But if there is ever a time in your lives where you need to do something, this is that moment. We need to get away from that guy as quickly as possible. To do it we NEED to hitchhike like we have never hitchhiked before! I know smiling is the hardest thing in the world to do right now but we need to do it, we need to look happy, we need to dance, and we need to find the energy to get the hell out of here."

We composed ourselves and pulled out our biggest smiles. We danced, I spun my fire balls and we desperately hoped that a ride would come. I had never feared for my safety or that of my sister and friend more than I did at that moment.

A taxi van pulled over. I thought, Shit, we can't afford a taxi! The driver got out and opened the back. "You know we're hitchhiking, right?" I asked. He said "Yeah, I know. I'm only going to Canmore, but you guys looked cool so I wanted to give you a ride."

"Thank you so much for pulling over! Now, I don't want to appear rude, but can I be totally honest with you?"

"Sure," the guy said, sounding surprised.

"See that guy down the highway?" I said pointing at the weirdo who was now riding his bike towards us.

"Yup."

"He followed us to the highway, he told us he has killed someone, he is clearly insane, possibly a junkie, and we are scared for our lives right now."

"Oh!" the man replied. Without a moment's hesitation he started throwing our bags in the van with urgency.

"Get in!" He said as he ran to the driver's seat.

We shut the doors and drove off just as the psycho approached the side of the van. The taxi driver swerved and ran him off the road without hitting him, then stepped on the gas. For a moment we were all silent.

The driver let us relax for a minute without saying a word. Then once we had composed ourselves, he asked us what happened. We told him the story and thanked him profusely for picking us up. It seemed like only a minute later he dropped us off in Canmore.

I looked down the highway and wondered how long it would take the strange man to ride his bike to where we were. I thanked the universe for sending us the taxi – the man had surely saved us. Then we waited along the highway for an hour with no luck while constantly watching to see if the psycho was biking towards us. It was one of the longest hours of my life. Time seemed to slow down while we talked over what we had just experienced. We all agreed that we had just been in grave danger. We hoped to get another ride as soon as possible.

After what seemed like forever, a black two-door Honda civic pulled over. The driver was named James and his girlfriend was Jan. Their trunk was packed full and there wasn't room for our bags and us.

"Well, it doesn't look like were going to fit," I said. "We can just wait for another ride. We don't want to trouble you, thanks for stopping."

"No, that's okay, we really want to give you a ride. We actually drove past you once already, stopped in a parking lot, rearranged the whole car and came back for you. So we'll find a way."

We laughed and thanked them again, but their trunk was packed full and it was clear we couldn't fit our bags in anywhere.

"We can just leave our camping chairs on the side of the highway," Jan said.

"Seriously, you don't have to leave your stuff for us."

But they insisted. "We want to hear about your adventure so we have got to get you in the car," Jan said simply.

Finally, after trying a few different ways of organising all the stuff in the car we managed to get everything in. That is with the luggage packed on all our laps, even Jan's in the front.

Once we drove off Jan asked, "So how has your day been?" We told them the story. James looked back at us and said, "That sounds super stressful, do you guys smoke?" My eyes lit up.

"When I saw Heidi's big blonde dreadlocks, I figured you guys probably did so when we repacked the car I rolled a big one to blaze with you." James then pulled out a massive joint the size of six one paper joints. "Hopefully this will make your day a whole lot better," he said with a wink before sparking it up.

I couldn't believe our luck. James passed it back and within seconds I could feel my entire body relaxing.

I have always believed that everything in the universe happens for a reason. I also believe that there are lessons in everything if you take the time to find them. I tried to find something positive out of the predicament we had just experienced and finally it dawned upon me. It was the first time that my sister had experienced the scary side of hitchhiking. It wasn't a good thing, but at least we were safe and now she knew why I had been concerned about her being on the road on her own. It was something for her to think about.

James offered to drop us off anywhere we wanted in the whole city of Calgary. We found a lake on the map and they dropped us off there. After many thanks, they drove away and we stood alone beside the lake. It turned out to be the water reservoir for Calgary. It wasn't the best spot but we were happy to be far away from all the stress of earlier that day.

RAY GUNZ
Calgary, Alberta. 6510 km.

"It is not the strength of the body that counts, but the strength of the spirit."
—J.R.R. Tolkien

We walked down the steep embankment to the edge of Calgary's main water reservoir. Swimming was prohibited, but it was hot and we didn't care. A little sign was not going to stop us from refreshing ourselves after a stressful day. After a cool swim we just sat in the sun to dry off.

"Wow, that was a pretty messed up situation in Banff eh?" I said trying to reflect on what had happened.

"Yeah, I would be happy to never be reminded of that again," my sister said.

I took that hint and pulled out my guitar. I sat and played my twelve-string at the edge of the water. Two guys and a girl made their way down the path towards us. One of the guys had a broken leg and dreads. He was being helped down the embankment by a young blonde girl. The other guy looked like Bernie from the eighties movie Weekend at Bernie's. They laughed the whole way down and when they finally made it to the bottom, they pulled out some beers. I made small talk with the group of people and when I saw one of the guys staring at my guitar I said, "Do you want to play it?"

"Really? I would love to," he said. "I haven't played a twelve-string guitar for years, it sounds amazing."

I passed him the guitar and he started playing and singing a Neil Young song. He was good. We chatted and laughed for a while with the strangers. Just as they were about to leave, the guy with the broken leg named Ray said, "Hey, do you guys want to crash at our place tonight? You're totally welcome if you're into it."

"Thanks for the offer, but we had a rough day and are happy to spend the night by ourselves," I said.

"You guys sure? You can have showers, do laundry, we can cook you some dinner, and we have tons of guitars you can play."

"Thanks for the offer, but we're happy just hanging here."

"All right, but we only live two blocks away, you can come check out our place and if you don't like it, it's a short walk back. Come on! It'll be fun!"

"All right, we will come have a look," I said after a brief discussion with the girls.

On the way we stopped at the beer store and I noticed that Ray knew the employee by name, but I couldn't tell if that was a good thing or a bad thing.

Around the corner from the store, we drove down a road and then pulled into a parking spot. Beside the driveway there was an old garage that we passed by before we went through a little gate into a small back yard. There were a few middle-aged guys drinking beers beside a barbeque. Without questioning who we were, they introduced themselves and made us feel welcome.

Ray gave us a quick tour of the house; the basement was set up as a recording studio and it had almost every instrument you could imagine. "Play anything you want to down here," Ray said, "you can crank the amps if you want to make some noise." After seeing all the instruments, I knew that we were in good hands. From my experience in life I had found that musicians were generally good people. I realised that they had probably invited us back to their house because I had offered Brad the chance to play my guitar. So we made ourselves at home and joined the other guys out back with some beers. Then we played guitar and told stories all night long.

The next morning, we cooked up a big breakfast and reminisced about the great night that we just had. When we started to pack up our gear Ray said, "Don't go just yet, stay for another night." After discussing it we decided that we really had nowhere better to be so we stayed.

That night got even crazier than the first and we laughed for hours and hours. The next morning when we started packing up history repeated itself. "Don't go, we had so much fun last night! Why don't you stay one last night?"

"We really can't," I insisted, "we have to be at the airport by seven tomorrow morning for Nicole's flight."

"Tell you what, if you guys party with us one last time I will personally drive you to the airport first thing in the morning," Ray said with confidence.

The offer was too good to refuse.

That night was the biggest party of them all and when it was four in the morning I finally snuck into bed just before my alarm woke me up at six. Ray was passed out in a chair in the living room and I had to shake him for a while before he finally woke up.

"Ray, we need to go or my sister will miss her flight."

"Take the truck out front," he mumbled as he handed me the keys out of his pocket.

"Dude, I might be able to get to the airport, but I will never find this place again," I told him.

"All right," he mumbled as he dragged himself out of the chair, "I'll drive."

We walked out to his blue Ford pick-up. When I looked in the back, I almost fell to the ground laughing. The bed of the truck was packed to the roof with empty beer cans. Literally packed! There must have been five hundred cases of empty beer or more. I finally realised why he knew the guy at the beer store so well.

There wasn't room for my sisters' bag in the back so I put it on my lap in the front. Ray pulled the truck into rush hour traffic and weaved in and out of cars. I was happy he did the driving, I didn't think I would find the airport if I had the whole day to look for it.

We made it a few minutes before my sister's flight was

supposed to take off. It wasn't looking good.

"Can you wait here? I'm going to go and see if I missed my flight or not. I'll be back if they won't let me board." Ten minutes later she returned – she had missed her flight and didn't have money for another one.

The last few days of partying had cleaned out most of my cash. I only had one hundred and ten dollars left to my name and my sister needed fifty to change her flight. I shrugged and gave it to her. "Good luck in school next year. Work hard. It'll pay off in the long run." We hugged and she went on her way. I thought of all the adventures we had gone on that summer and was happy to have a sister as cool as Nicole. I was sad to see her go, but happy she was going to keep studying.

Some people used to always tell me that I was lucky when good things happened to me. But I always told them that I wasn't lucky, I had worked hard to achieve my goals. I hoped that Nicole would continue working towards her goals and find whatever she is looking for in life.

When I got back to Ray's house, I started packing up my tent. I didn't know where I was going to go and I didn't know what Heidi wanted to do either. We had many decisions to make. My plan was to check out a few ski resorts in B.C. in an attempt to decide where to live during the approaching winter. But it was hard to get around without a car or money and I hadn't done any research in the towns I had made it to already. We had gone through Nelson, Revelstoke, Golden, and Banff and I knew nothing more about any of them.

My sister had mentioned going to Alaska and the idea intrigued me so I pulled out the map and looked at all the possible routes to take. By the time I finished packing up my tent, Heidi and I had agreed to go to Alaska. I was nervous when I thought about going so far north and a voice in my mind asked, why do you continually take the hard road?

It was a good question.

GOING TO ALASKA
Canmore, Alberta. 6615 km.

"You will become like the people you hang around with."

It was late August and the Canadian summer was coming to an end. Each day was a little bit colder, the leaves on the trees were changing colour, and the animals were preparing for their long hibernation. It was not the best time of year to go north, but we had made up our minds. Heidi didn't have much either, so we set ourselves a budget of twenty bucks a week. That gave us three weeks to get to Alaska and back before we ran out of money.

Ray's friend dropped us off on the highway going north and after a short wait a middle-aged couple named Suzy and John gave us a ride back up to Canmore.

"Where are you headed?" Suzy asked.

"We're going to try to make it up to Alaska," I replied.

"Alaska! It could snow any day up there this late in the year, maybe you should reconsider."

"We'll be fine," I assured her.

"Do you have enough money? And winter clothes?"

"Yeah, we should be good." I figured we would be okay on our budget and she didn't need to know that we didn't have any proper winter clothes.

"Here, I want you to take this," Suzy said, while she tried to pass a twenty to us.

"No, seriously – we will be fine. We have enough money, were just doing it for the adventure."

We didn't want people's money or donations, we just wanted to see how far we could go with almost nothing.

"Please take it," she begged. She looked like she was going to cry. "Even if you don't need it, we just want to contribute something to your adventure. Spend it on having fun." We regretfully accepted the money.

When we arrived in Canmore, Heidi and I stashed our bags in some bushes so we wouldn't have to carry them around all night, then wandered around the little ski town. We found a bar that had an open mic night so we went inside. Since we had that extra twenty dollars, we decided to spend it on a few beers. It was nice to go to a bar without our bags and to feel like a normal person, even if it was just for a night. It reminded me of the countless evenings at university I had spent at bars with my friends and for just a moment I felt like I was back home.

We milked our single beer over the course of the night. When the bar finally closed, reality struck again. We walked back down the cobblestone path and over a little bridge. Then we searched for our bags that we had stashed in the bushes. It was a little hard to find in the darkness, but eventually we located them.

The next morning I ate a peanut butter sandwich while I watched some backpackers cook up a gourmet breakfast behind their van. I knew I wasn't going to be eating much over the next few weeks, but I was happy that I had any food at all.

When we got back on the highway, I secretly hoped that we would get a ride through Banff. We got a ride with two elderly people named Jack and Sally in a brand new Cadillac. They drove us past Banff and dropped us off at the turnoff to Jasper. When we got out of the car, Sally said, "You know, it's a bit too late in the year to think about going north, it could snow any day now. It would be a better decision to stay near the border where it's warmer – you're welcome to come further with us if you like." But we had made up our mind to go north. Sally gave us a big bar of dairy milk chocolate in case we got hungry. I could never turn down chocolate, especially from a grandma.

The highway north was a small two-lane road with no cars to be found anywhere in sight. I looked around at the evergreen trees that lined the side of the road. The air was cooler and I knew that the temperature would continue to drop with each day that went by. We had a long scary road ahead and almost no money. On top of that I was travelling with someone that I didn't actually know that well. I felt more alone than ever before and once again I wondered what I was doing with my life.

I could easily get a job and enjoy a comfortable life just like everybody else. It was so simple. But I knew that in every job that I had ever worked, I eventually stopped learning and got bored. I knew that I was chasing something, something more fulfilling. I knew that people who didn't set a goal to achieve in life felt lost. I imagined that I was similar to them. I didn't know what I wanted and I didn't know where to look for it. But until I figured out a path for my life, Alaska seemed like the best direction to go. I just hoped that I would make it back alive.

THE BURNT HOUSE
Jasper, Alberta. 6822 km.

"If somebody upsets you, they are in control of you."

We stood on the highway at the entrance to Jasper National Park. There were toll booths blocking the road ahead and the park entry fees were posted on a large sign. There was no way we could afford them. I hoped that the toll booths were closed when we got a ride.

I again wondered if our trip to Alaska was a bad idea. We had already been told by two people not to go. Should we have listened to the warnings? Or should we follow our own path in life? The last year had turned out to be the best year of my life and everyone had told me not to go then as well. I looked down at the laminated map and tried to use the legend to estimate the distance to Alaska. It looked like it would be at least 3000 km. If we travelled a hundred km a day it would take a month; if we went five hundred km a day we could be there in a week.

No cars passed for hours, then a pick-up slowed down as

it approached us. A guy named Jim was driving and he seemed nice, so we took the ride. As he pulled up to the toll booths, they waved him through. It turned out that he had a yearly park's pass attached to his truck. I was relieved.

A short while later a bird hit the windshield and ricocheted off into the ditch. Jim didn't blink an eye lid. "Did you notice that bird hit the window?" I asked, wondering why he didn't react at all.

"Oh yeah, I saw it. There are so few cars on this road that I hit birds every time I drive this way. It's sad, but they just aren't used to cars around here." We drove past a gully that looked like it had been carved out of the mountains by the glaciers. Eventually we arrived at the edge of a glacier, it was massive but visibly receding.

When we arrived at the turnoff to Jasper Jim dropped us off. It was a few kilometres up the road to the town centre and after seeing how few cars were on the roads we decided to just walk. Jasper was nothing like I had imagined it would be. It was a small town surrounded by fields, dead centre in the middle of a big valley. There were no trees or bushes we could find to camp in and we wondered where we were going to sleep that night.

We found an information booth in a park and got a map of the local area. It confirmed our suspicions of there being no good spot to camp anywhere nearby. We decided to take advantage of the daylight and search the town for a place to lay our heads.

After looking with no luck for some time, we found a burnt-out two-story house surrounded by police tape that had a fenced-in back yard. We knew straight away that we weren't going to find a better place for the night. When the coast was clear, we snuck into the back yard. It looked unkempt, but the fence blocked any view from the neighbour's windows – perfect. We stashed our bags under some bushes and then snuck out of the derelict property.

We explored the town full of boutique restaurants, fancy shops, and rich tourists. We were dirty, scruffy, and our clothes were well worn. It was clear that we didn't fit in. We walked past a posh restaurant and a table of people pointed at us like we were monkeys in a zoo. I walked up to the window, looked in, and pointed at them in response. I wished I hadn't. I knew that if someone upset me and made me react, that they were in control of me.

I saw a poster on a telephone poll looking for volunteers for a festival that coming weekend. I wanted to take down the number but I didn't have a pen or a phone. We decided to get the number on our way out of town the next day.

It was starting to get dark and it was already clear that the town had nothing to offer us, so we went back to the burnt-out house and set up our tent for the evening. It was nice to be sleeping in a backyard. It gave me that feeling of being at home. Maybe it was the security of the fence around us that assured me that there was nothing to worry about. No bears, no people, just the safety of the yard.

I lay in bed wondering what Alaska looked like. I doubted that we would be allowed across the border since I had heard that the US officials were very strict. But I still thought it was worth trying. If we made it that far and they didn't let us in, I figured we would just have to turn around.

ROBSON VALLEY
MUSIC FESTIVAL
Dunster, B.C. 6964 km.

"Set your intention on where you want to go, and you just might get there."

Heidi and I woke up early, packed up the tent, and walked back to the highway, hoping to make some distance. Only a few cars passed by the whole morning and we wondered if we were going to get a ride at all. At last in the mid-afternoon a small four-door Honda civic pulled over and a young couple hopped out to say hi.

"Where are you guys headed?" I asked, hoping that they were going north.

"We're going to a music festival in Dunster, B.C."

That was the moment I realised that we had forgot to get the number for volunteering at the festival off the poster in Jasper. I was pretty sure it was the same festival.

"We were going to try to volunteer there, we just saw the

poster yesterday but forgot to get the number."

"Well, you can always come with us and see if you can work something out."

"Thanks, that sounds like a great plan."

Tom and Stacey were both nurses from Calgary and were volunteering as first aid attendants at the festival. We chatted the whole way there. When we arrived at the front gate, a lady was putting up some signs. Tom got out of the car and talked to her. It turned out that she was the festival organiser. Eventually he mentioned that he had a few hitchhikers in the car who were interested in volunteering.

The look on her face went sour. I jumped out of the car and went to introduce myself.

"I'm willing to do anything," I said "Clean toilets, garbage collection, I will literally do anything that's available."

"Well honey, we just don't have any jobs left. You might be better off applying earlier next year."

My heart sunk, but I kept my composure. It wasn't over yet. I thought that getting a ride straight to the festival had been a good omen.

"That's all good, thanks anyway. I was just hoping to play guitar, since I had heard that there were great jams around the campfire every night and I brought my twelve-string guitar with me."

At that her eyes lit up.

"A twelve-string?" she asked, "Can I see it?"

"Sure," I replied.

I went to the trunk and pulled out my guitar, a beautiful Cort with a cutaway for soloing. Her facial expression changed dramatically again and for a second I thought that we might have a chance.

"Well, maybe we can find you something to do. Why don't you go and set up in the campground for the night and we'll let you know tomorrow? If we can find some work, you can stay, but if we can't you can at least camp tonight for free."

"Thank you so much!" I replied. "If you find us a job, I won't let you down. And if you don't, thanks for the place to sleep tonight." Tom and Stacey went off to set up their tents at the medical station while Heidi and I went to the campground.

At night people made one big fire in the middle of the campground. Anyone who had instruments brought them to the fire and we made music late into the evening. The next day the organiser came to our tent and let us know we would be on garbage and toilet duty and to report for work the next morning. I was stoked – another festival was a great way to start our journey to Alaska.

When I arrived for work the next morning, the organiser introduced me to a man with long white hair, a white moustache, and a mellow vibe.

"This is Bill, you'll be working with him all weekend so follow his instructions."

"All right Matty, today we've got to put garbage cans around the festival, we've got a lot of work to do. But I think that first we should have a safety meeting. Follow me."

I followed him into a little shed and waited for him to pull out some safety material to read. He fiddled around in a drawer then said, "Why don't you have a seat on that little crate?" I sat down and waited patiently to hear about the rules for onsite safety. I was surprised when he pulled out a pipe instead of paperwork. He packed it full of fragrant bud and hit it like a champ, then he passed it to me.

"Ha ha ha, I thought we were actually going to have a health and safety meeting!"

"No, not around here man, it's just a term construction worker's use when they want to get high," he said with a grin.

Any doubts I had about garbage duty quickly vanished – with Bill it was going to be fun. After another pipe we loaded the back of an old pick-up truck with trash cans and set off.

"Hop in the front," Bill said. I pulled open the passenger door and watched as it almost fell off. It was only held on by one hinge.

Bill just laughed, "Don't worry about that, it's been broken for a while."

Once inside, Bill flipped a light switch that was attached to the truck near the gear shifter. "That turns on the fuel pump," he said before he fired up the old truck.

We dropped the bins off around the festival site. In the campground we walked past a group of guys sitting in lawn chairs who were having a safety meeting of their own. Bill stopped dead in his tracks and said, "Follow me." He walked up to the group of guys and said, "Look guys, we're on garbage duty and our job is to ensure that the safety requirements are up to standard on site, so we are going to have to join your safety meeting." Everybody laughed and someone passed him the joint. Bill took a few big drags and then he passed it to me, and after a few puffs I passed it back into the circle.

"Thanks for doing the dirty work and come back for a smoke anytime you want," our new friends said as we walked away. It was obvious that Bill was there to have a good time. Once we put the rest of the bins out, we got a load of toilet paper. I dreaded the thought of cleaning out filthy porta potties, but surprisingly there were none. There were only composting outhouses and they were all very clean. We stocked up the toilet paper in all the outhouses and that was it.

"Come find me around five and we'll go around and empty the trash before nightfall," Bill said before he sent me on my way.

I walked back to my tent stoked. My job was way easier than I had imagined it would be and we were at a great festival. The music had started, the campground was filling up, and it looked like there was a good weekend ahead. I didn't know where Heidi had gone so I went for a wander around and found her chopping vegetables in the staff kitchen.

"Hey, what are you up to?"

"I got a job helping out in the kitchen!"

"Oh, nice. Do you need any extra help?" I asked the lady in charge of the kitchen.

"That would be wonderful, we are so far behind on our prep work."

The kitchen was cooking food for all of the musicians

that were playing. I was put to work chopping potatoes and carrots and I munched away as I worked.

It was a smart move on Heidi's part. We were budgeting only twenty bucks a week for food and as a result we had not been eating very well. When we finished all the prep in the kitchen, the lady offered us something delicious to eat and told us to come back anytime we were hungry. We thanked her and told her we would see her very soon. Every time we went for food, we helped out in the kitchen first – sometimes we did dishes, sometimes prep, and sometimes we helped cook.

The next three nights were amazing. The festival had one small stage with a large variety of musical acts. The crowd was intimate and friendly. It was a great place to be. When I was back in the campground sitting by the fire playing guitar, people kept passing around little treats to enhance each other's experience. It was a great place to be and I was very happy that I had brought my twelve-string hitchhiking.

When the festival ended, I knew we would be back to life on the road. The festival provided the highest of highs but I knew that the road could provide the lowest of lows if I didn't think the right way. It seemed as if it would be easier travelling if we didn't have such good experiences, because we would have nothing to compare the bad ones too. Much like life. But I suppose there is something to be learned there. If I could just be content with whatever I get, life would be so simple. It is the desire for more that seems to complicate it.

A HOME FOR THE NIGHT

Mackenzie, B.C. 7391 km.

"If dreams were real and reality was a dream, how would you know the difference?"

When we hit the road to hitchhike, it was obvious by the empty lanes that not many cars would be going by. I wondered if there would be even less as we got further north. Eventually a middle-aged man named Michael picked us up in his Subaru wagon.

We drove through Prince George where we passed the infamous Highway of Tears. A seven hundred and twenty-km corridor where more than forty female hitchhikers have disappeared since the early 1970s. Although we weren't taking that highway, I knew we shouldn't let the fact slip our minds. It was a testament to where we had arrived. A place where murders and missing person cases had been unsolved for decades. The people who committed the crimes were still on the loose and potentially lurking somewhere nearby. We continued on highway 97 north, the empty highway was lined with evergreen trees and nothing else. With no visible buildings in any direction, it was easy to see how someone could disappear without a trace around there.

I felt that with each kilometre we travelled further north, our risk of disappearing grew. We had left society behind long before and now wide empty space replaced it. There was no help readily available if we needed it. In truth, the only help we might be able to get was from each other. As long as we both weren't overpowered in some way, survival seemed plausible for at least one of us. That is unless a family of hungry bears found us.

In the car things were more upbeat than the themes I was pondering in my mind. We were with a nice person and chatting about meditation.

"Have you ever heard of astral travelling?" Michael asked, bringing me back into the here and now. When I shook my head he continued, "It's when you leave your physical self and have an out-of-body experience. With practice you can go anywhere you want in the universe and observe what's happening. But it's dangerous and the further you travel, the harder it is to get back to your body."

"So you astral travel?" I asked.

"Yes, I've been doing it for years. With practice it becomes easier, but it's always risky."

It seemed like a crazy concept – leaving your body and travelling across the universe, but I had read about it before so I didn't doubt what he told us.

Surrounded by wilderness, I knew that we were no longer at the top of the food chain. There were no farms, no shops, and no people. Michael invited us to stay at his place for the night. Staying with strangers was against my rules, especially with all the stories of hitchhikers going missing in northern B.C., but Michael seemed trustworthy and I couldn't see a better place to sleep besides the forest, which was surely full of bears.

Since I was breaking some of my hitchhiking rules, as a precaution we decided to not eat or drink anything that Michael offered us, just on the off-chance that he tried to drug us. We arrived in the little town of Mackenzie B.C. where we pulled up to a small house with light blue siding. Michael gave us a quick tour of his home and showed us the extra room in the basement that we could sleep in. It was pitch black. The windows had been covered so that no light got in, but he explained that it was the room that he did his astral travelling in.

I remembered that I had some bud left over in my bag from the festival.

"Do you smoke?" I asked Michael.

"Well, not very often but I'll have a toke with you if you light one up," he replied.

I rolled one and we went out back to smoke it.

"I've got to confess," Mike said, "it's actually quite hard living in such a small town. Everybody gossips about each other's business. I just don't fit in around here, so it's nice to hang out with you guys for a change. The only reason I stay is because I love nature and the hiking is great around here."

"Well, we're glad you picked us up – it's been fun hanging out with you. We have food and can cook some dinner if you're hungry?"

The munchies had definitely kicked in.

"That would be wonderful," Michael replied with a smile.

It was obvious that he appreciated our offer as much as we appreciated his hospitality. It was nice to sleep in the comfort of a bed again, something I hadn't done for months. In the morning Mike drove us back to the highway.

"It was cool to hang out with some people who accept me for who I am," he said when he dropped us off. We thought the same thing.

CRAZY TRUCKERS
Chetwynd, B.C. 7568 km.

"Rules only exist for those who follow them."

There was no doubt about it – we had arrived in the north. We left the rest of the world far behind and replaced it with an empty road and infinite expanse of evergreens. We really were in the middle of nowhere where hours could go by without us seeing any cars. I wondered if it was an omen of things to come. Surely if there were so few cars on the road to Alaska, there was a good chance that we would never make it there? But perhaps we were just on a road that didn't have many cars. There was no way to tell. We waited for six hours in the cold autumn air, watching the world slowly go by. Eventually a pick-up truck pulled over, and just like a week before it was full of people. The driver offered us a ride if we were happy to sit outside in the back, which we gladly accepted.

We had just jumped in when the driver floored it, spinning the tires and almost losing control of the truck on the gravel shoulder, skidding only inches away from the ditch. Heidi and I looked at each other, worried that we had made a bad choice. But the driver yelled, "Sorry," out the window then cautiously drove off, slowly accelerating until he achieved his desired speed.

The air was noticeably cooler and we didn't have any warm clothes to wear. I didn't know what we would do if the temperature dropped below zero so I just let the thought pass. A while later we arrived in Chetwynd, B.C., a small town in the middle of northern B.C. We hopped out at the only set of stoplights in town.

There were still a few more hours of light left, so we decided to try to get another ride before it got too dark. We walked across the street just past the stoplights and dropped our bags on the side of the road. I noticed a liquor store behind us and I thought about how nice a cold beer would be, but I didn't have the money.

There were more cars driving through Chetwynd than there had been back in Mackenzie. Just as the last light left the sky, a big transport truck pulled into the parking lot of the liquor store. The driver ran inside and then just as quickly ran out with a paper bag in his hand.

We watched as he got back into his truck, turned on the engine and pulled out of the parking lot onto the road as fast as the truck would go. He was gaining speed quickly and pulled out into the intersection just as the lights turned yellow.

I was confused. He had his right-hand signal on, but had driven past the right-hand turn lane and into the centre of the intersection. I thought that perhaps he had just decided to go straight on. Then to my surprise the truck started turning right. It was obvious that he wasn't going to make it around the stoplight with his truck, but he didn't slow down. His trailer hit the stoplight and I jumped as it came crashing down in front of us. The light exploded on impact with the ground and sparks flew everywhere. Heidi and I grabbed our bags and ran. The truck didn't stop, but instead continued to speed up while each wheel on its trailer crunched over the wrecked stoplight lying in the road. The intersection was blocked and people got out of their cars in shock and disbelief, while the truck drove on like nothing had happened.

A car pulled over and asked if we had taken down the license plate, but it had been the last thing on my mind when we were running for our lives. I was thankful that we had not been standing closer to the intersection.

Nobody chased after the truck, even though I could still see its taillights in the distance. Things were obviously different up north. I hadn't seen a police car in the last few days and I had the strange suspicion that we were more on our own than we had imagined. For the rest of our journey, it seemed our decisions alone would determine our fate.

FLAMES ON A TRUCK
Chetwynd, B.C. 7568 km.

"Sometimes you get what you want before you know you want it."

The next morning when we were hitchhiking on the side of the road a man from the house behind us walked over.

"Where are you guys from?" he asked.

"Toronto," I replied.

"You know it's a bad time of year to go north? It could snow any day now up here," he said. I just nodded. "Are you in a rush? Or do you have some time to come and tell me about your journey? I would love to hear about it."

With nothing better to do we walked into the man's back yard and sat down with him. He was a Native American and we chatted about life.

"Here, I have some candied salmon for your journey," he said as he handed us a bottle full of fish.

"I caught the fish the traditional way, with a spear, and we used every piece of it so nothing was wasted."

The salmon didn't look very appetising and I thought

186

that there was almost no chance that I was going to eat any of it, but I didn't want to be rude.

"Thank you," I replied.

He reminded me of the Native American code of ethics that I remembered reading on a wall when I was back in Tofino. They have a certain respect for nature and people that no longer seems to be part of our world today. We walked back to the road while I wondered what to do with the salmon. Camping with fish in the tent in bear country didn't seem like a good idea. Maybe I will eat it, I thought.

A white pick-up truck with flames painted on the side drove past us and I wished he had pulled over. What could possibly be better than riding in a truck with flames on the side? Then a moment later the truck slammed on its brakes and came to a grinding halt on the side of the road ahead. He was already pretty far from us and I wasn't sure if he had stopped to offer us a lift or for something else. But we saw him wave out the window at us. We jogged towards the truck with our bags and were greeted by a big smile from a big burly man.

"How far north are you going?" I asked.

"Just to my turnoff, an hour or so up the road. I can take you there if you want? My name's Grant."

We hopped in the truck and we drove off. Grant worked at a mining camp two weeks on and two weeks off. He just started his down time and was on his way to meet his family at his cottage.

"You want a beer?" he asked.

My eyes lit up as he reached behind the seat and stuck

his hand into the cool box of beer.

"You like to puff?" he asked next.

"Oh yeah," I replied.

"All right, how about I drive while you light them up?" he said with a big grin before pulling out a bag with at least thirty pre-rolled joints in it. I was again realising that things were different up north. There were no police to enforce the rules, so people did what they wanted.

Grant slammed on the brakes. I looked around worried, but it was only because he had spotted a beer store. He went in and grabbed another case and then we kept drinking, chatting, and smoking joints until we arrived at his turnoff. He let us out at Dawson Creek, B.C. and before he drove off I gave him the candied salmon, sure that I was never going to eat it.

Across the street from where we stood was the Dawson Creek historic village. It looked like it was from the early 1900s – old cars and buildings dotted the landscape from a bygone era. We wandered around the place, then went to find a spot to hitchhike. I looked up at the sign in front of us and it said, 'Mile 1, The Alaska Highway.'

It felt as if one adventure had just ended and another was about to begin. A newfound optimism seemed to awaken within me with the thought that we only had one more road to go before we arrived in Alaska. It seemed so close even though it was still almost 2000 kilometres away.

THE ALASKA HIGHWAY

Dawson Creek, B.C. 7669 km.

"You have not lived today until you have done something for someone who can never repay you."
—John Bunyan

The landscape looked brown, dusty, and dirty, a big change from the lush green colours of the forests we had been through only a day before. Actually being on the Alaska Highway brought us hope and optimism. We had made it to the road we wanted to travel. We only needed a few good rides and with luck we could be at the Alaska Border in a matter of days.

Most of the vehicles that drove past us were pick-up trucks and I realised that they were probably the only cars that could make it anywhere in the winter as far north as we were. But there were lots of them, which was a change from the empty road we had stood on only a day before. Even though the roads were busy not one person stopped to pick us up.

Eventually a truck pulled over on the side street behind

us and a guy called us over. We grabbed our bags and dashed towards the truck. But when we got there the man behind the wheel said, "Sorry I can't give you a ride or any food, but I wanted to help you guys out in some way." He then pulled out a handful of cash and said, "This is for you."

"Oh, no – thanks for the offer, but we don't actually need any money, we have lots," I lied. I wanted to tell him that we're just doing it for the adventure.

"Look, it doesn't matter to me if you need the money or not. I just wanted to do my good deed for the day. If you don't need it, just take it and go have some fun with it. It would make me happy."

The guy wouldn't take no for an answer, so we reluctantly accepted the money.

"Have a good trip, stay safe!" he said before he drove off.

We were still within our budget of twenty dollars for the week, since we had eaten most of our meals at the festival. However, the man's eighty buck donation gave us a whole new sense of security. We would at least be able to feed ourselves until we got back home.

I smiled at every car that went past, willing someone to give us a ride and after a while a truck pulled over with a young guy named Tim behind the wheel. We threw our stuff in the back and we hopped in the front of the cab with him. We had just started on the Alaska Highway when traffic slowed down and then ground to a halt.

"I know a faster way," Tim said, and he did a U-turn. He drove back in the direction we had come from, then turned down a road that we had just driven past. I was a bit suspicious at first, but after about thirty seconds on the road we took another turn and continued in the same direction we had been going, just on a different road.

Tim floored it and we hit one hundred and twenty km/h as the truck raced down the gravel road. "We're passing that whole line of traffic right now," Tim said in his northern cowboy's accent.

"So what do you do for work?" I asked.

"I'm a mechanic, I work on the oil rigs. It's a pretty good job, but in the winter the temperature drops below minus fifty. We don't turn off our trucks the whole winter if they're outside – it only takes a minute for the fuel lines to freeze. In fact, it's so cold that you get instant frostbite if your skin is exposed to the air. We can only stay outside for short periods of time when we work in winter."

We turned onto the main road again where Tim merged into the traffic then drove over the Peace River.

There was a little town called Taylor, B.C. just after the bridge and Tim dropped us off at the shops there. We continued to hitchhike and as I watched the cars drive by, I realised that they were the same ones that had passed us in Dawson's Creek. They must have all been stuck in the traffic jam that we had skirted around. I could see some bewildered looks on people's faces as they tried to figure out how we could have possibly ended up on the road ahead of them and I couldn't help but laugh.

I was happy that we had covered some distance on the Alaska Highway. It seemed as if our destination was finally within our grasp instead of just a dream. As long as the cars kept coming we would get there eventually.

RUSTY
Taylor, B.C. 7725 km.

"Sometimes it is better to live in the moment than worry about where you're going next."

I had trouble getting the advice offered by our rides out of my mind. Every single one up to that point had told us that it could snow in Alaska any day now. I wondered if we were making a big mistake. If it snowed there would be no room to hitchhike on the road. We would surely be stuck and I didn't have money for a bus. I was torn between trying to make good decisions and the thrill of exploring the unknown. The pleasure of adventuring seemed to keep overtaking good decision making. I hoped that it wasn't going to catch up with us.

After waiting for hours in the hot sun, we decided to refill our water bottles at the bar across the street. I waited outside with our bags while Heidi went in. As I stood there a man wearing a cowboy hat and boots walked up and said, "Howdy."

His truck was parked right in front of where I was sitting and he fiddled around with stuff in the back while he made small talk.

"Hey, how are you doing?" I replied.

"Good, just getting some supplies. Looks like you're on quite the adventure. Any good stories?"

"Yeah, quite a few actually."

"Well, that doesn't surprise me," the man said. "You headed north or south?"

"North."

"Whooeee, a little late in the year to be headed in that direction. You have some warm clothes?"

"Uh, yeah… a few." I lied.

Heidi returned, "Well, we had better get back to hitching if we're going to get a ride by the end of the day."

The man, who was still within earshot, spoke up, "Where are you planning on spending the night?"

"As far north as we can get," I replied.

"Well, I've got a stew cooking over the fire back at my place right now, you're welcome to come camp for the night and have something to eat. There's plenty if you're hungry. My place is just on the edge of the Peace River. By the way, the names Rusty," he said before shaking our hands.

"Sounds good to us." A hot meal was too hard to turn down. I knew I was breaking another one of my hitchhiking rules but Rusty seemed like a nice guy.

When we got in his truck he drove south, in the opposite direction that we wanted to go. I wondered if we should have just continued hitchhiking, but it was already too late.

Rusty pulled off the Alaska Highway onto a gravel track that ran along the edge of the Peace River. There were fishing boats trawling in the murky brown water. Rusty pulled into a campground and parked next to a big old school bus.

He and his wife were the campground managers and they called the bus home. Beside it there was a large pot full of bubbling stew hanging over a fire, just like he had promised. Rusty gave us a tour of his bus. The old seats had been taken out and replaced with a kitchen, a wood stove, a widescreen television, and a bed with leopard print covers on it.

Rusty's wife wasn't home when we got there. "Things haven't been going so good between my wife and I," Rusty told us, and the glamour of his set-up seemed to fade away. It wasn't a living situation that was going to impress everybody, but with the right person you could be content.

"You guys know how to make chapatis?" Rusty asked.

"No, but were happy to try if you teach us."

"All right, I'll help with the dough, then show you how to make the first one, after that you guys can make the rest if you like. Chapatis are a simple flatbread made with flour, water, salt, and oil."

He threw the simple ingredients into a bowl and mushed them up until he had a dough, then he took out a handful and rolled it thinner than a pancake.

"Voilà."

We got to work and when we had finished making a pile of them Rusty served up the stew. Then we ate while sitting around the fire.

After dinner Rusty brought out his guitar. That was the moment I realised that he had probably invited us back because I had my guitar. We spent the rest of the evening playing music beside the campfire. The temperature gradually dropped with each hour that passed and we were forced to move closer to the fire to stay warm.

I had been breaking more than a few of my hitchhiking rules. That night was the second time we had gone to stay at someone's house. This time we barely knew the guy. We just went back with him after a brief conversation. But my last hitchhiking rule was to follow your instinct. In the short conversation I had with Rusty, I felt that he was trustworthy. I guess we were just lucky that he was a good guy. In the morning he dropped us off where he had picked us up the day before.

GUNS 'N FEAR
Taylor, B.C. 7725 km.

"Poor decision making will almost always lead to less than desirable outcomes."

We waited more than half the day for a ride but nobody seemed to want to stop. When we saw a blue GMC pick-up truck pull over we knew it might be our only chance to get a lift all day. There were four guys inside the truck and when we walked up to the window, one of the them said, "We're drinking beers and taking the back roads." We should have taken the fact that they were drinking as a warning, but it was starting to seem normal up north. Anyway, they sounded like they were having fun.

There just weren't enough cars pulling over so far north and as a result our standards for accepting a ride were dropping. But when you're broke, and need to cover some distance, you got to do what you got to do.

We put our bags in the back of the pick-up truck while the guys re-arranged themselves. Three of them sat upfront so Heidi and I could fit into the back with the other guy. After a few kilometres we turned off the highway and onto the back roads, just as we had expected.

The guys gave us a beer and we drove away. After a while the driver started driving a little bit more recklessly than he had been before. It was alarming but the further north we were, the more drunk and stoned the motorists seemed to be so I tried to shrug it off.

We had all been making small talk for the first part of the ride until one of the guys up front said in a hushed voice, "We're in the middle of fucking nowhere now, nobody would ever find them here." He followed the comment with a weird laugh and all the other guys laughed along with him. Things had gone from good too bad in a matter of seconds. I wondered what we could do to get out of our predicament. But we were already so far off the highway driving down back roads with no signs, that the thought of asking to get out seemed almost as bad as staying in the truck.

The three guys up front continued talking under their breath and I heard the word "rape" followed by more laughter.

I stared ahead down the long empty road wondering what we had got ourselves into, while wondering how we were going to get out of it.

"Look what I found," one of the guys up front said as he pulled out what looked like an air rifle from under the seats. I shuddered at the sight of it and wondered if it actually worked. "Where's the ammo?" he asked.

"I don't have any," the driver said. "Well, let's go get some then."

I didn't like the sound of the way things were going.

"You can't say we didn't warn you we were taking the back roads," one of them said before snickering.

"Hey, let's go by my house and grab my big gun!" another said.

We were worried to say the least.

They were more drunk than I had at first imagined and I knew it was in our best interests to get away from them as quickly as possible. But getting dropped off on a dirt road in the middle of northern B.C. did not seem like a great idea. Their comments got worse and they started to speak loud enough for us to hear them. They seemed to be getting more confident with their taunting.

"They'll never find you out here," one said.

"There are four of us and only two of you, who do you think is going to win?" said another. The comments were quickly turning into threats. I thought about the options I had for survival. Four on one were not good odds, but if it came to it and we had to protect ourselves, I wouldn't back down.

After zigzagging down some dirt tracks we pulled into a residential area then parked outside a house. It seemed like an ideal time to get out and run but we had no idea where the highway was and didn't want to get stranded there. One of the guy's ran inside the house to get his gun.

"Should we run?" Heidi whispered.

"Yeah probably, but I have no idea where we are."

"I know, me neither."

It was too late, the guy had already returned with a

shotgun in his hand. My heart felt like it sunk to the bottom of my stomach. We were a second away from jumping out of the truck when the guy with the gun said, "I don't have any ammo, we're going to have to stop by the shops."

A sense of relief flooded through my whole body. 'No ammo,' was the best possible thing we could have heard. The knowledge that we were going to go to the shops added another layer of security to the situation. If we were actually going to go, it would probably be the ideal time to escape. But only time would tell if we had made the right decision.

We pulled out of the driveway and again zigzagged through the residential area while I wondered if he actually needed ammo or if it was a bluff to keep us in the car. Should we have jumped out already? Was it now too late? Had we made a huge mistake not taking the only chance we had to escape? Every second that passed seemed like eternity. The laughter had stopped and things seemed more tense than before. Had our luck run out? Surely things had escalated seeing as there was now a shotgun in the truck, regardless if it was loaded or not. Every threat I had heard along the ride now seemed more real. Why did we take the ride? I thought.

Then when we pulled back onto the Alaska Highway I was relieved to say the least. We were in a little town, there were people, cars, and trucks around. If only we would stop. Then we pulled up to a gun store. Without a moment of hesitation Heidi and I jumped out of the truck, grabbed all our bags, and ran. The guys in the truck all laughed, but I remembered that we were in the part of Canada where people disappeared without a trace. Serial killers were still on the loose. Maybe those guys were joking, maybe they weren't. But up north where people make their own laws, they had given me no reason to believe that they had good intentions.

"I'm so glad to not be in that truck anymore." Heidi said.

"Yeah, me too. Things went downhill pretty quick in there. We should probably be a bit more careful with our rides from here on out."

"Yeah, for sure. That was super sketchy. Especially when they pulled that little gun out in the middle of nowhere and were saying that messed up stuff."

"Yeah, I know. Well let's just be a little more careful next time."

That ride was a warning for us. A warning to choose our rides wisely, the next time we may not get a chance to escape. I thought back to my rules and the reasons I had made them in the first place. After countless nice people picking us up, dropping our guard was an easy thing to do. But if we did not change our ways we would end up in trouble sooner or later.

We found a sign that told us we were in Fort St. John, B.C., and we walked to the side of the road and waited. I watched the guys come out of the gun store with two boxes of ammo while they laughed. It made me sad to be a human.

THE HOMELESS SHELTER
Fort Nelson, B.C. 8124 km.

"We are products of our past, but we don't have to be prisoners of it."
—Rick Warren

It felt good to be back on the road, away from guns and people with bad intentions. We decided to pick our rides more carefully from that point onwards. Our next ride was with an older guy named Gary, who was driving a new white pick-up truck and had a big smile on his face when he pulled over. He seemed like a better ride choice than the last guys, so we got in. He told us he was an executive in the oil industry and working on a few projects in the area. We felt safe in the car with him.

Halfway to Fort Nelson Gary pulled over at the only building that we had seen for hours. It was a little restaurant and we went in. When the waitress came to the table, Gary said, "Get anything you guys want, it's on me."

"Thanks, but were not hungry," Heidi and I both replied.

"Ah, c'mon guys, get something. If you're not hungry you can just take it with you."

Heidi and I looked at each other. We were trying to live off our budget as a challenge. But then Gary said, "Seriously, anything you want."

"Okay, we'll grab something, thank you," we replied. I thought that maybe he wanted us to eat too so he wouldn't be eating alone. Heidi and I ordered some food and then Gary just ordered a coffee. I was in disbelief, but I realised that he just wanted to buy us lunch.

After a few more hours of driving we got dropped off in Fort Nelson, one of the last towns in B.C. before the Yukon. There wasn't much to the town, it looked more like a stopover for truckers on the long drive north. We waited until sunset for a ride, but not many cars passed by and nobody stopped for us.

Eventually a light brown Chrysler van pulled over with an older lady behind the wheel. I walked up to the window stoked to get a ride, but she quickly squashed my hopes. "Sorry honey, I can't give you a ride, I just wanted to tell you that if you don't get a ride soon there is a homeless shelter a few blocks away. They've got beds, showers, washing machines, and they give you food vouchers for Subway." She gave us directions and then drove off.

Staying in a homeless shelter was not on my list of things to do in life. In fact, I didn't even consider it as an option. But the temperature was a lot colder than it had been and it was getting dark. The thought of eating a proper meal instead of peanut butter sandwiches was tempting me more than I had imagined it would. So after accepting that we weren't going to get a ride, we decided to give the shelter a chance. We walked into the industrial area where the lady had directed us. Trucks were pulling in and out of driveways and it didn't look like there was a shelter anywhere. In fact, it didn't look like there was anything inhabitable, just big grey warehouses.

Then we saw a little white house with a light on outside that seemed like the only inhabitable place in the neighbourhood. We walked up to the door and knocked, and it was quickly answered by an older man with thin white hair.

"Can I help you guys?" he asked, looking us up and down.

"Uh, we heard there was a shelter around here, but I don't know if were at the right place."

"Oh, of course – come in, have a seat. We have some beds available but you can't sleep in the same rooms, the facilities are separate for men and women. This is a drug- and alcohol-free shelter and you will be evicted immediately if you break the rules. If you can just fill out a few forms I can show you around."

I looked at the form, which asked our names, age, date of birth, where we were from, height, weight, hair colour, etc. – it read like a form for missing people. I realised that there must be a few people who went through the shelter that were never heard from again.

"Each day you are entitled to breakfast, lunch, and dinner at Subway." Even though we had just arrived, he gave us our vouchers for the whole day. A total of twenty-five dollars, broken down into five dollar coupons. It was more than our weekly budget for food.

"There are showers, a laundry machine you can use, and bags full of clothes if you need anything warm. You know that it could snow any day up here, right?"

When we finished the forms, the man showed us to our rooms. I was sharing mine with an older guy who looked like an alcoholic. I decided it would be better if I just kept to myself. Heidi and I took our coupons and went for dinner. It was nice to have so much money to play with, we felt like millionaires. I got a sub, a Coke, and a whole bunch of cookies and I still had vouchers left over for the next day.

When we got back to the shelter Heidi started rustling through the bags of clothes the man had offered to us for our journey north. She found some men's long johns that looked like they would fit me. "You want these?" she asked.

"Nah, I have never worn long johns in my life and I don't plan on starting with someone else's."

"Well, I'll take them for you anyway, just in case," she replied. I found a sweet pair of red wool socks that looked like they were knitted by a grandma, so I grabbed them just in case. I tried to remember the last time I had washed my clothes and I couldn't. In fact I couldn't remember the last time I had a hot shower either. So I went to have one. It felt amazing, I appreciated it more than ever before. The water was warm, soothing, and seemed to calm my wandering mind.

When I got into bed, I stuffed all of my important

belongings into one of my socks, then put it under the covers with me. I went to sleep early, partly to avoid talking to the sketchy guy in the room and partly because it had been a mentally exhausting day on the road. I stared at the ceiling and wondered if we were going to make it to Alaska. Everybody kept telling us it was a bad idea, but for some reason my mind would not be changed.

In the morning there was a different man at the shelter's reception and he asked if we were going to stay another night. The thought was tempting, but with each day that passed it got a little colder, so we decided to hit the road instead. Before we left, he gave us another full day's worth of vouchers for Subway. On the way out of town we filled our bag with as many subs and cookies as we could buy.

We tried a few different spots to hitch from on the highway, but none seemed to work any better than the others. So eventually we gave up trying and just sat on our bags and waited. An older guy with a big moustache like Wyatt Earp and a cowboy hat pulled over and greeted us with a smile.

"Where you headed guys?" he asked.

"Alaska."

"Well, I'm heading up to the Yukon and can take you as far as I'm going."

"Great, thanks!"

We jumped into the truck and the man introduced himself as Jerry and his girlfriend Tegan was beside him.

"You guys smoke?" he asked.

"Yep," I said with a broad grin. It seemed as though

everybody was either drinking beers or smoking buds up north.

"Well, you better get to work rolling then," Jerry said with a smile before he passed a big plastic container full of weed to me. I looked at it and estimated it to be at least an ounce of what he told me was Sour Diesel. I wanted to try to buy a bud from him, but I just didn't have the money. I rolled a big one and passed it up front for Jerry to light but like a true stoner he said, "you do the honours," and he tossed me a lighter. The first few puffs were magical and all my worries quickly disappeared.

"Where in particular are you guys headed anyways?" Jerry asked.

"Oh, we just want to explore Alaska," Heidi said.

He turned around with a bemused look upon his face and said, "You know it might snow any day now up in these parts?"

"Yeah, we heard about that, but we want to at least try to get there," I said.

"You guys got any bear spray?" he asked.

"Nope."

"Bears are preparing for hibernation at this time of year and eating anything they can. If you can afford some bear spray, it would be a real good investment."

It seemed as though every person that picked us up said the same thing. It was like listening to a broken record. I knew that they were all just trying to keep us safe, but I wanted to have some fun and see somewhere that I hadn't been before. With our request, Jerry dropped us off at the

Liard Hot Springs located somewhere desolate near the Yukon border.

It was the most remote place we had been to yet. Hundreds of kilometres separated us from any reasonably sized town and it was clear the we were right in the depths of bear country. If anything went wrong we would surely be stranded. I could not even begin to imagine how long an ambulance would take to arrive if we needed one. But I suppose it didn't matter. We didn't need an ambulance and I hoped that wouldn't change.

HOT SPRINGS AND BUFFALO
Liard River, B.C. 8429 km.

"When you move lower on the food chain, your perspective of what matters changes quickly."

We had planned to camp right beside the hot springs, but when we walked off the road towards them our hopes were crushed. It turned out that they were actually within a campground and we would have to pay to stay. That was not going to work for us on twenty dollars a week so instead we looked up and down the road for somewhere else to camp. We saw a gravel parking lot across the street that had a few camper vans parked in it so we decided to check it out. When we got closer, we saw some people eating dinner around a campfire beside their motor homes. We said hi as we walked past, then found a patch of grass in the corner of the lot to put up our tent. Once we were set up we went and joined the people around their campfire for a bit of warmth, then retired to bed in our tent on top of the soft, comfy grass.

The next morning a strange voice from outside the tent

said, "Good morning."

"Good morning," I replied as I unzipped the flap, wondering who was there.

It was the little old lady that we had chatted to the night before by the campfire and she had brought us hot chocolates to warm us up after the cool night. It was a great way to start our day.

We drank our drinks while we slowly packed our bags. It had been cold at night and I was happy that I had got the big red socks from the shelter as I would have been frozen without them.

Once we emptied all of our stuff out of the tent, I folded it, squeezed all the air out, and began to roll it up. However, when I rolled the first bit over I realised that the whole bottom of the tent was covered in animal excrement. We had camped on top of the biggest pile of poo that I had ever seen. At last I had discovered why we had such a comfortable sleep. I looked around and tried to figure out what type of animal could have left such a big pile, but I had no idea and I didn't really want to find out.

I knew that if I didn't clean the bottom of the tent, when I rolled it up the whole thing would be covered in poop. With no cleaning materials at my disposal, I decided to use clumps of grass to wipe it off. After a while, it looked almost as good as new.

We crossed the street and paid our five bucks admission to get into the hot springs. We walked through the campground and along a boardwalk over a bubbling brown steamy swamp that was nothing like anything I had seen before.

The pools were surreal, steam rose from them in the calm frigid air. We soaked in the pools until our skin was water logged and our bodies were relaxed. There is no better feeling than sitting in hot water in the cold northern air while the birds chirped away around us. When we were content, we made the trek back over the boardwalk and onto the highway.

When we got to the road, I was sure that I could see a herd of giant animals grazing in the distance but I was unsure of what they were. I went up to the ticket booth and asked, "Are those buffalo along the highway?"

The ranger replied, "Yup, they just cross the highway back and forth to eat grass all day long." I couldn't believe it. I had no idea buffalo still roamed free. I thought they had all been killed a long time ago.

When I got back to the road, Heidi said, "Shit, I forgot to take a picture of the hot springs. Are you happy to wait with our stuff while I go?"

"Sure, go for it. If I get a ride I'll try to stall them for you."

She grabbed her camera and ran off after promising that she would be as quick as she could. I sat and stared at the buffalo, and just like the ranger said they crossed the highway back and forth, moving a little bit closer each time. I got excited at the thought of seeing one up close. I wondered if I was going to be in their way and if I should move our bags somewhere safe, but I decided to wait and see where they went. Surely they could just walk around me if they got close.

Their actual size became more noticeable when they got closer and I guessed that they must weigh at least 2000 pounds each. They gradually advanced, crossing the road back and forth until they were only a hundred metres away from me. It seemed like the spot I was standing in was quite likely the next place that they were going to head for. I wanted to move, but it was already too late. We had way too many bags for me to carry on my own, so I decided to stand my ground.

Yet as they got closer, I realised that there was a giant flaw in my plan. There were at least fifty 2000-pound wild beasts headed in my direction and it appeared as if I was in their way. I was just a scrawny one hundred and eighty-pound stick of a human up against a gigantic pack of animals. The clock was ticking and I didn't know what to do. Our bags were our life, if they got trampled and destroyed our trip would be over. But it was too late to move. I saw the first few buffalo start walking in my direction.

Then all of a sudden I heard the screeching of tires as an old brown pick-up truck came racing out of the campground towards the herd. Then it did a U-turn as it passed by and slammed on the brakes in front of me. The driver jumped out and shouted, "Throw your bags in the back and get in." Before I had bent over, he had already thrown the first of our stuff in the back of the truck. I didn't have time to think, I just did what he said and seconds later I was in the truck with him pulling off the highway and into the campground.

It was the park ranger. "Son, you were about thirty seconds away from getting trampled. Those are wild animals, you had better be careful next time." He stopped the truck in the entrance of the campground and then pulled out a gun from behind his seat. I was shocked and tried to figure out why he had pulled it out.

He saw the expression on my face and said, "Don't worry, they're only blanks. Come with me, the show is about to start. Part of my job is to keep the buffalo out of the campground so they don't trample people in their tents."

We watched the heard of buffalo milling around where I had just been standing. "Here we go," the ranger said. He held the gun high in the air then fired, BOOM. The ground began to shake and the sound of thunder filled the air as the buffalo began to run past us at full speed. The ranger fired again and they ran even faster. It was quite the spectacle. Their size and power were breathtaking and I became absolutely sure that I was nowhere near the top of the food chain in the north.

Once they had all stampeded past the campground, they slowed down and started grazing again like nothing had ever happened. Heidi came back and wondered what the loud noises had been. She had missed the show. We grabbed our bags from the back of the park ranger's truck and headed back to the road.

The sky was a crisp autumn blue and the leaves on the trees had already changed colour and would soon drop. The only thing that was missing on our trip were cars driving north. I had only counted five and some trucks going north the entire morning, yet lots seemed to be heading south. I wondered if it was a sign that the season for adventuring in the north was coming to an end. There was a truck stop on the other side of the road and a few drivers had pulled in for food, but they all drove away shortly after.

Since I had started hitchhiking, I had been hoping a trucker would pick us up like in the movies, but not one had slowed down the whole trip. After Heidi and I discussed our options we decided that it would be worth asking truckers at the truck stop if we could get a ride with them.

So when the next truck pulled in, we watched closely as the driver got out, ran into the restaurant, and then came back out, ready to get back on the road. The truck was carrying large cement tubes and metal beams on the back and we saw that the driver was walking around checking that they were all still fastened securely.

We approached him slowly and introduced ourselves. Then after a bit of small talk we asked the magical question, "Is there any chance we could get a ride up north with you?" I could see the wheels turning in his head while he looked us up and down.

He unenthusiastically said, "Yeah, I guess I can give you a ride. But you know it's a bad time of year to go up north, right? It can snow any day now."

"Yeah, we know."

"All right then, where are your bags?"

We grabbed them from the side of the road and he helped us load them into his truck. His name was Blair and he looked like he had driven a lot of miles. Heidi hopped on the bed in the back and I sat in the passenger seat.

"I used to drive a truck back in Ontario during my

summers at university," I said, trying to break the ice.

"Oh yeah? What kind of truck?"

"Just a heavy rigid. I delivered Pepsi. It paid well, but we delivered the whole load by hand. It was pretty tiring."

"Yeah, I try to stay away from too much physical work these days so I just do long haul. Been doing this route for years. Up to Inuvik in the Arctic then back down south." The conversation flowed and after a while we were even joking around. Sitting in the truck so high off the ground allowed us to get a great view of the rugged uninhabited terrain that surrounded us.

"We're in the wild now guys, if anything goes wrong with the truck it could be days before a tow shows up."

I sincerely hoped that would not happen. In fact I was hoping that he would take us all the way north with him, it would be cool to say that we had crossed into the Arctic Circle. We crossed the border out of B.C. and into the Yukon. We had entered the land of the Yukon Gold potatoes that I had been eating since I was a kid. Whitehorse, Yukon's capital, was our next stop.

We drove for hours without passing a single house, property, rest stop, or store. We really were in the middle of absolute nowhere. Road work signs started to line the highway that said, 'Expect long delays ahead.' Then when we finally arrived at the road works, we were told we would have to wait at least half an hour. Up ahead I could see that the road was covered in shattered boulders leftover from blowing a cliff apart on the side of the highway. Large machinery worked quickly to move the rocks out of the way, but the road was covered with them so I could see why it was going to take a while.

I remembered that I had a little bit of bud stashed away in my bag so I asked Blair if he wanted to smoke. He said, "No, sorry man – I can't smoke while I'm driving. But feel free to go blaze one beside the truck if you want, it don't bother me none." I was stoked. I rolled one up and had a puff beside the truck, then got back in and chilled.

When they finally let us through the road works, Blair reached under his seat, pulled out a bag, then threw it on my lap and said, "Start rolling dude," with a big grin on his face.

I laughed and said, "oh, so you do smoke?"

"Yup, just not in front of people. But we can smoke in here now." I laughed again as he tossed me a pack of papers and said, "make it a big one, we've got a long drive ahead of us." I rolled up a fatty and when I was done he told me to light it up. By the time the joint was finished, I was well and truly stoned.

I had just reached the peak of my high when Blair looked at me anxiously and said, "Did you hear that?" But I didn't hear a thing. "There it is again," he said insisting that something was wrong. Then when we started to climb the next big hill the truck lost most of its power and we barely rolled over the top of it. "I'm going to pull over at the next possible spot, something's gone wrong."

My nightmare of getting stuck in the wilderness with no cars on the road, no civilisation, and lots of hungry bears appeared to be coming true. A short while later we saw a gas station with its windows boarded up and Blair pulled the truck into the parking lot. He got out and opened the engine and I followed, offering any assistance that he might need. "Well, it looks like the truck blew a fuel line," Blair said. He got his tool box out and started undoing a little metal hose.

I desperately hoped that he could fix the problem, as I didn't want to get stuck where we were.

"Hop in the truck and turn it over if you can," Blair said. I climbed up the steps and sat behind the wheel where I followed Blair's instructions.

He got me to turn the truck on and off over and over again while he tried to fix the line. Once it was turning over he got me to rev the engine and then he told me to come back down. Then he jumped up in the cab and started revving the engine before climbing back down again.

He looked at me and said "We have two options, either we wait here for a tow truck, which could take anywhere from eight hours to two days depending on where it is, or we try to make it to Whitehorse, but we might lose a hundred litres of fuel along the way." My heart raced while I waited for his decision.

He said, "Well, let's see how far we can make it," so we got back in the truck. My high was completely destroyed. Heidi got in the front and I sat in the back and again questioned my life choices. When hitchhiking was good, it was great, but when it was bad it was horrible. The further we went, the less power the truck seemed to have.

Eventually, we arrived at the outskirts of Whitehorse and Blair pulled into a little gas station, the first we had seen the whole day that wasn't out of business. It was the place that he had hoped to make it to as they had a wrecker's yard in the back.

The lights outside were all turned off, but there was still someone working in the garage. Blair went to say hi and it seemed as if they knew each other. After a few minutes Blair said he was going to look for a part and a short while later he returned with the news that he had what he needed.

"Are we able to keep going north with you? We were thinking of trying to get to the Arctic Circle."

"Well, if I take you any further north you are most likely going to get eaten by a bear. There is nothing for you up there and just by going you're putting your lives on the line, especially this late in the year. So it's probably best if we part company here." We looked at the map and decided that if we did get into Alaska, we could go up to the Arctic Circle from there. We thanked Blair for the ride and wished him luck on the rest of his journey.

Heidi and I grabbed our stuff and headed into the bush beside the parking lot. It was the first really cold night on our trip and I was happy I had the big red socks I got from the shelter. Heidi gave me the long johns she picked out and it was so cold I didn't care who had worn them before. We even snuggled to share body heat, just to stay warm.

The next morning the air had an icy chill to it and all the condensation on the tent had turned to ice. When I looked outside the ground was white and covered in frost. I was starting to understand why everyone had told us not to go so far north so late in the year. But we were so close to Alaska.

Bears began to worry me a bit more every day, partly because we were camping in their territory and partly because we didn't have bear spray to protect ourselves. I knew that the bears this far north didn't have much contact with humans, so to them anything that moved was a potential meal. On top of that it was the time of year when the bears were trying to put on weight for hibernation.

We knocked the ice off the tent and then packed it up. After some breakfast we went back through the gas station parking lot towards the road. Blair was under the hood of his truck, covered in grease while a big chunk of his engine sat on the ground.

"Good morning, do you need any help in there?" I asked him.

"Nah, I'm all good thanks. But I think you should reconsider going north this late in the year. It's really not a good idea."

"Thanks for the advice," I said before we walked to the road.

I was happy that we had made it to Whitehorse. The thought of getting stuck back down the highway when the fuel line on the truck broke was almost too terrifying to think about. I knew we weren't prepared for the situations we could face in the wilderness. I just hoped that we wouldn't see any bears. It really was wild in the north and each day we seemed to just sneak by. It was as though we were always just one step away from mortal danger. I hoped that it would remain that way.

IT'S COLD OUTSIDE
Whitehorse, Yukon. 9077 km.

"What good is the warmth of summer, without the cold of winter to give it sweetness."
—John Steinbeck

The cold wind sent a chill through my body. It was clear that winter was coming. A jacket for warmth would have made sitting on the side of the road more bearable, but you can't always get what you want. After waiting for a few hours an old blue Buick pulled over and gave us a lift into the centre of Whitehorse.

Being in a city felt safe and I realised why homeless people chose cities. There was a degree of comfort, safety, and familiarity that isn't available when you're alone in the woods. But after thinking about it for a while, I realised that maybe the comfort of the city came from the awareness that we wouldn't get eaten by a bear. At least while we were there.

Heidi and I walked up a big hill that led to the highway. I knew that we were getting close to the Alaskan border and that any ride that picked us up could take us there. I decided to stash the rest of my illegal goodies in a hole I dug beside a fence, not wanting to show up at the border with them. I didn't think I would ever find them again, but only time would tell. If I did ever make it back to Whitehorse, I would at least have a treasure hunt ahead of me.

At the top of the hill a sign said, 'The Alaska Highway' and cars were racing by. I was pleased the roads were full of cars again, as it was a nice change from the other side of Whitehorse. After waiting for a few hours we got a ride one hundred km up the road to Haines Junction.

BRAVE OR CRAZY?

Haines Junction, Yukon. 9231 km.

"If you are unwilling to change and adapt as your situation in life changes, life will always be one step ahead of you."

A grizzly bear statue welcomed us to the little town of Haines Junction, another sign that told us we were deep in bear territory. The town had a bar and a few little shops for tourists, but nothing for us. We waited the whole day on the side of the road while staring at the grizzly bear, the only one we hoped that we would see.

Just before the sun set, we wandered into the forest to find a place to put up our tent for the night. Most of the leaves had already fallen off the trees and the bushes had pale yellow ones that would surely fall off the next time the wind blew. The air was cold, so we decided to make a fire for warmth and a hot meal. Then we set up our tent on top of an embankment that overlooked a valley.

I went for a wander through the grasslands where I was scared a bear might be lurking in an attempt to deal with my fear of them. I convinced myself that there was no point in being scared of bears since we were probably never going to encounter one.

Then I walked back to our tent without a worry in the world. That night was even colder than the one before and I wondered how much colder it was going to get.

In the morning we got a quick ride twenty minutes up the highway from a local guy. As he was dropping us off on the side of the road, the guy said, "You do have bear spray, don't you?"

"Uh, no," I replied.

"Well, if you get stuck here tonight your best bet is probably to break into that old cabin over there. No one lives in it and it's probably a safer bet than getting eaten by bears. Just a few days ago a local guy was jogging through the woods and got attacked. It's just that time of year."

"Thanks for the tip," I said.

"That's all right, just make sure you get some bear spray the next chance you have."

We stared at the cabin that he had pointed too. It didn't seem like breaking and entering was a good idea, but getting eaten by a bear seemed a lot worse. I looked all around us, but there was nothing to see – no people, no cars, just nature and the abandoned shack. The longer we stood there in the cold air, the more appealing the little shack became.

A light brown Ford pick-up truck pulled over that had an older couple up front. We walked over to the window

"Where are you headed?" I asked.

"To Alaska," the lady replied, "we can take you as far as the border if you like."

"That would be amazing, thanks." At last, we had a ride to Alaska!

The man's name was Harold and his wife's name was Beatrice. They had come up from the lower States, crossed the border into Washington, and were hoping to make it to Fairbanks, Alaska, by nightfall to meet their grandchild.

We talked for hours on the road and I couldn't stop thinking about what might happen at the border. Would the border patrol let us just walk across? Would they send us back to Canada? Had I gotten everything illegal out of my bag? If we made it across would we be able to get a ride on the other side? There were too many possibilities of what might happen.

Harold pulled the truck over at a rest stop near Beaver Creek in the Yukon. It looked like it hadn't been used in years. We walked inside the shop that seemed more like a living room than a store. The walls were covered in little trinkets for tourists including rocks, crystals, and semiprecious gemstones of all sorts. By the counter there were shelves of food, covered in a thick layer of dust that must have sat untouched for years.

I looked at the food they had for sale and it all seemed to be from another era. There was even a 'whole chicken in a can' that must have been at least twenty years old. I wondered if they would actually sell it if someone wanted to buy it. I looked for an expiry date, but there wasn't one. I could not believe that at some point in the past people actually bought whole chickens in a can.

Harold and Beatrice knew the people that owned the

shop and they sat down for a coffee together. They reminisced about the hunting trips they used to go on years before. I wondered if they brought whole chickens in a can with them on those trips. Heidi and I went back outside and sat in the parking lot. After a while Harold and Beatrice came out and we continued along the Alaska Highway. It was the final leg of our journey to the border and I secretly hoped that Harold and Beatrice would take us across with them.

CROSSING THE
BOARDER ALASKA, USA
Canada/Alaska Boarder 9564 km.

"If you tell the truth, you don't have to remember anything."
—Mark Twain

The Alaska Border sign stood high and proud. Just reading it made me feel like our trip had been a success. I knew being allowed to cross was beyond our control. I was nervous and waited for Harold to drop us off before the checkpoint, but he didn't. Instead he pulled into the border with us still in the back. Within seconds of the truck stopping a US border patrol agent walked up to the window. He was tall, fit, walked with a straight back, and had a serious look on his face.

"How does everybody in the vehicle know each other?" he said. It was the first thing that had come out of his mouth and he had already divided us. Harold responded, "This is my wife, and we are giving these guys a ride to Alaska."

The border patrol looked at us in the back. "Would the two hitchhikers please take all of their belongings out of the vehicle and bring them into the office?"

Heidi and I grabbed our stuff and thanked Harold and Beatrice for the ride.

They both said, "We will wait for you."

"It's all good," I replied, "you don't have to wait. We appreciate you taking us this far."

"Oh, it's no problem. We'll be here," they assured us.

"Okay, we'll be as quick as we can."

We started to walk towards the office but before we entered the border patrol agent asked, "Are you sure you grabbed everything that belongs to you out of the truck?"

"Yes."

"Okay."

I couldn't see through the tinted office door, so I opened it up and inside there was a counter with another guard standing behind it.

"Could I see your passports please?"

We passed them over and then waited while he punched our names into the computer. I was surprised that he was checking them as I thought we would have been rejected straight away.

Then the questions began: "What are your names?" "Where do you live?" "Do you have any tobacco, firearms, or weapons?" "Do you smoke?" "Why do you want to go to Alaska?" "How long do you plan on staying?" The questions went on and on.

"Could you open your bags please?" He looked into mine

first and started rummaging through it. He unravelled my clothes, went through the pockets and looked in every little spot he could find.

"Are these your rolling papers?" he asked me.

"Uh, yes."

"What are they for? I thought you said you didn't smoke."

He caught me off guard, I either had to lie and say that I did smoke and destroy all my credibility or I had to tell the truth.

"Oh, I don't smoke tobacco," I replied

"What do you mean?"

"Ah, back in Canada I like to smoke… something else sometimes."

"What do you smoke?"

I didn't want to say. I knew weed was illegal in Canada and the US in 2008. If I admitted to smoking it, I would be admitting to doing something illegal. But I was in too deep and I figured honesty is always the best route to take.

"Weed," I said sheepishly, while still wondering if it was a good idea to share that information or not.

"And do you have any on you?"

"No, I left it in Canada."

"When's the last time you smoked?"

"A few days ago," I replied.

He grabbed a handful of my clothes from the counter and put them back in my bag before he said, "Just so you know, by admitting to taking drugs I am legally not allowed to let you across the border."

My heart sank. I had just blown it for Heidi and myself

by being honest. The expression on my face went sour and I started stuffing my belongings back into my bag.

"So that's it? We're not getting into Alaska?" I asked.

He purposefully coughed and said, "I don't think you heard me correctly, I said just so you know. That is the law. You will not be permitted to enter the United States if you admit to using drugs, ever." Then he gave me a little smile and started going through Heidi's bag. I didn't quite know what was happening so I just kept quiet. I finished repacking my bag and stood there while he went through Heidi's stuff.

When he was done with Heidi's bag, he put two little forms on the counter and said, "You will have to fill these forms out for your entry visa and pay five dollars each."

I could not believe that he was letting us through. The guy looked scary and acted like he ate nails for breakfast but he was actually a genuinely nice guy. "Enjoy Alaska," he said as we walked out the door.

I was surprised that we had actually made it into Alaska. Two weeks earlier it seemed like just a dream that we were talking about. Since that conversation we had travelled almost 3000 kilometres, yet we hadn't covered one kilometre in Alaska. We had a long way to go, more aware than ever that we were still not safe in the wilderness.

NORTHERN LIGHTS AND A LYNX

Fairbanks, Alaska. 10,023 km.

"When something is important enough, you do it even if the odds are not in your favour."
—Elon Musk

True to their word, Harold and Beatrice were still waiting when we walked out the door. When we got inside their truck, we thanked them again for waiting and then they drove off.

"Well, now you've made it where were you planning on going first?" Beatrice asked.

"We hadn't thought that far ahead," I replied. "I really didn't think we were going to get across." We all chuckled.

"We're headed up to Fairbanks and are happy to take you there if you like."

We had made it into Alaska. Into a place that had almost twice the missing person rate as the rest of the USA. Was making it across the border a good thing or a bad thing? I wondered as I looked at the map and followed the long winding road from the border to Fairbanks. There wasn't a single town in between and the road was long. Had we pushed our luck too far? What would happen if it actually snowed? I knew there wouldn't be room to stand on the road to hitch and besides that, it would be too dangerous. Camping on top of snow was out of the question as hypothermia would be guaranteed.

I saw a family of moose standing by a pond just beyond the edge of the road and they momentarily took my mind away from my negative thoughts. The sun was setting beyond countless evergreen trees and there were no houses or buildings anywhere to be seen. I was starting to realise how big, empty, and wild Alaska really was.

I leaned my cheek against the truck's window and I could feel an icy chill from the other side. It was the coldest night yet. I stared out into the darkness wondering what we should do next. But as I stared off into the night I became quite sure that the sky was becoming brighter. Soon, fluorescent green rays of light shined vertically through the sky as if they were sent from another universe. Harold pulled the truck over onto the side of the road and we all got out and looked up at the magnificent northern lights. We stood in the chilly night air and watched the once in a lifetime event.

Sometime later we pulled into Fairbanks, where the streetlights were decorated like giant candy canes and the whole city seemed to be ready for Christmas... even though it was only August.

"Wow, they sure get ready for Christmas early up here," I said.

"Well it is where Santa Clause lives," Beatrice said with a smile. We turned off the highway onto a smaller dirt road. It was pitch black, but I wasn't scared. We had spent the last ten hours in the truck with Harold and Beatrice and I knew they were good people. As we drove down the track looking at house numbers a lynx walked in front of the truck, then stopped. It looked up at us, its yellow eyes glowed like fire and then it dashed into the bushes.

We pulled up a driveway and were greeted by Harold and Beatrice's children. They offered us a room in their house, but we kindly declined not wanting to intrude. We did however accept the offer to camp in their yard.

We set up our tent in the cold night air while we stood underneath the northern lights. We took the cover off the top of the tent and got inside. Then we watched the northern lights from the comfort of our sleeping bags, which was magical. I wondered why we kept getting offered places to stay. Was it just down to the fact that we had met such nice people? Maybe it was because I had a guitar? Or perhaps people thought we were going to get eaten by bears?

Seeing the northern lights was a dream come true and I smiled while I looked up at them from inside the warmth of my sleeping bag. They were majestic and beautiful like green rays of sunlight piercing through the dark night sky. Although the road we chose to take in life was rough and scary sometimes, it kept making my dreams come true and as long as that kept happening I was going to keep on following that road.

THE NORTH
Fairbanks, Alaska. 10,023 km.

"When you are unable to tell those closest to you your secrets, a life full of friends can seem empty."

Sunshine warmed our thin canvas tent. When I woke up I looked around and remembered that we had made it into Alaska. I heard a noise and when I looked out of the tent I saw a brown-haired girl sitting on the veranda who I hadn't met the night before.

I got up and introduced myself, and the girl told me her name was Erica. After a bit of small talk, she said, "I'm going into town in a little while, I would be happy to give you a ride to the highway if you like."

"That would be amazing," I replied, "thanks."

A short while later we got in Erica's Jeep and drove off.

"So, where ya'll planning on going next?" she asked.

"Well, we were thinking of trying to get up to the Arctic Circle."

She looked at us in disbelief then blatantly said, "That's a terrible idea! Just yesterday two people were camping up there and got eaten alive by a polar bear. They even had a shotgun right beside them in their tent. Bears are desperate to put on weight before hibernation at this time of year and there was a bad berry season this year. There just isn't enough food for them to eat. As a result they have been attacking humans all around Alaska. You do have bear spray, don't you?"

I looked at her sheepishly and said, "No."

"Well, if there are two suggestions that I can make for you to get back to Canada alive, one would be to get some bear spray as soon as possible. The other would be to not go to the Arctic Circle, since you will quite likely not make it back."

She looked serious. I could tell she had doubts about our safety in Alaska.

"Actually," she said, "I need to go to a store that sells bear spray, I can take you with me if you like?"

"Okay," I replied. It couldn't hurt to have a look, I thought.

We walked into the store and browsed the bear spray section. The cheapest bottle was thirty dollars, almost all of our money. I did the math in my head and it just didn't make sense. If we bought it and our trip back south took longer than expected, we could both be broke and hungry.

We decided to take our chances with the bears. It seemed like the most logical thing to do. I really didn't want to be stuck in Alaska with no money. I pulled out the map and looked at the different routes we could take.

Now that the Arctic Circle was out of the question, we

had the choice of either going west or back to where we had already come from.

When Erica finished shopping, she asked, "Did you get some bear spray?"

"No," I replied, and I could see the look of worry on her face.

I really hadn't thought that we would make it into Alaska in the first place and was unprepared for the situations that we might face. I thought about the extra money the man gave us in Dawson Creek and how we could have spent the rest of it on the can of bear spray, but it was too late. We were already back in the Jeep on our way to the highway.

For a few minutes, we sat in the truck in silence. I thought it was because Erica was upset that we didn't get bear spray. But then she spoke, "Guys, can I tell you something personal that I really need to get off my chest?"

"Sure," Heidi and I both replied.

"I just found out I'm pregnant from a one-night stand. On top of that there is not one person in the world I can tell because everybody I know is super religious and very anti-abortion. I haven't decided what I am going to do yet but I don't want to raise a child without a father."

Tears rolled down her cheeks as she spoke. We tried to console her as best as we could.

"Have you talked to the guy about it?" I asked.

"No, not yet. I don't know what to say. I don't even know the guy, it was just a night of fun."

"Well, maybe talk to him and then go from there," I suggested.

"Yeah… I suppose that's the best thing to do."

"Follow your heart and do whatever you think is best for you," Heidi said.

I wished that there was something more I could do or say, but our time together was brief and we had already arrived at our drop-off point.

"Thanks so much for listening to me," she said after we got out, "I feel better already now that I have at least got it off of my chest and had some advice."

We hugged her and wished her all the best. I was sure that she had offered us a ride so that she could tell us about her situation. We must have been the only opportunity she saw to talk to someone about it. It seemed like she had been waiting for us when we woke up. But I was happy to help her in any way I could, even if it was just by listening. Once again, I found it odd how people shared their deepest secrets with strangers but I guess it's because we're probably never going to see each other again.

Before she drove away, she said "Now, ya'll don't stay in Alaska too long, ye hear me? It could snow any day."

I stood there on the side of the road wondering if we should have bought the bear spray. We probably should have spent the money we had on it. But it was already too late – we had our warning but we didn't take our opportunity. We could only hope that we weren't going to need it.

HUNGRY BEARS
Denali National Park, Alaska. 10,224 km.

"It is better to die than to have never lived."

It was our first day alone in Alaska and although not many cars had gone by, we were both feeling optimistic. I knew that each ride we got would be crucial to our survival as we ventured even further away from civilisation without bear spray. Only trees lined the sides of the highway and surely the creatures of the forest were not far away.

A jolly looking old man pulled over in a brown SUV. He rolled down his window and asked, "Where are you headed?"

I pointed down the highway and said in a sarcastic tone, "That way."

He chuckled and said, "Well then, hop in."

The man's name was Rob.

"How far are you going?" I asked, wondering where we might end up.

"Well, I'm going all the way to Anchorage, but I'm going

to stop to do a wildlife tour at Denali National Park along the way."

"Cool, what's Denali National Park like?" I asked.

"It's the biggest natural wildlife park in Alaska and home to the highest mountain peak in North America. Miles of land untouched by humans, except for one road through the middle of the park for the tourist buses. You're guaranteed to see all sorts of animals in their natural habitat – caribou, grizzly bears, black bears, mountain goats, wolves, and everything in between."

Rob showed us where it was on his GPS. I stared at the large green space that outlined Denali National Park and wondered if we should go as well. We arrived at the park mid-afternoon and Rob drove us straight to the tour centre where we parted ways. The tour cost fifteen dollars each and luckily we had the extra money that we didn't spend on bear spray.

We booked the first tour we could get on and paid for the ticket, then went outside and got on the big blue school bus just before it drove off. It took a single lane dirt track and almost as soon as we got out of the trees into an open plain, we saw the first of many grizzly bears – a mom with her two cubs walking casually in the long grass.

The bus drove slowly through the grasslands and we stared at the majestic peaks of Denali Mountain that lined the horizon – it was the tallest mountain in North America. The grizzly walked close to the bus with her two cubs. A little while later there was another grizzly, the biggest we had seen yet. Every once and a while we would pass another tourist bus as we made our way further into the park. We saw a herd of caribou grazing in a field. A little while later we saw a lone wolf. Then we saw more grizzly bears. It was amazing to see so much wildlife, but the thought of having to camp with so many bears in the area was daunting to say the least. I wondered if all of Alaska had as many bears as we had seen on the tour. If so, it would explain why everybody was so worried about us camping without bear spray.

When the tour finished, I read in the tourist office that where food is abundant, bear densities can be as high as one per square mile. Heidi and I walked back to the road. We both wanted to get to some sort of civilisation as quickly as possible but the sun was already dropping in the sky and we hadn't checked out what the town had to offer.

We walked along a bridge over a river that roared below us. We explored the small row of shops that were clearly all intended for tourists. We thought of camping behind them, but there was a steep embankment and it didn't seem like a good spot.

I saw a payphone and went to call my mom on a long-distance phone card I had bought before I left. I picked up the receiver and put in my mom's number and eventually I heard ringing on the other end.

"Hello," said my mom.

"Hi mom!"

"Hi Matthew, how are you?"

"I'm good thanks. I made it to Alaska! I'm in Denali National Park!"

"How did you get there?" she asked.

"I hitchhiked."

The conversation went sour. She was still not pleased about my decision to go hitchhiking. It was not exactly the chat I had hoped to have. I knew that she was just a concerned mom and I was her little boy out in the world. We said our goodbyes but I wished that I hadn't called. All I wanted to say was hi and tell her that I was okay.

I thought of how nice living back in Whistler would be. At that moment if I was in Whistler I would be living in a house with running water, heat, electricity, and would be surrounded by my friends. I would spend the summer days with my buddies skateboarding around town, playing guitar, and swimming in the lakes. It sounded like the perfect life. But I quickly reminded myself that if I didn't go hitchhiking that first time, I would never have made it there. I could be living in a city, working in an office, staring out of my window and day dreaming of places I would never visit.

I reassured myself that I was there for a reason. To change, to grow, to learn, and to push through my fears, regardless of what they were. I told myself to suck it up, to be strong, and to keep my head up high… at least until I made it back to Whistler.

I managed to clear my mind again and I looked around me. I was in a beautiful place on the adventure of a lifetime with a cool friend and plenty of time to spare. I thought about what people must go through when they get old and look back on their life. Surely some wished that they had done more with their time. I just hoped that I would be happy with the choices I made in my life whenever that moment arrived for me.

We walked back down the street and then trekked into the bushes to look for a spot to camp. Eventually we found a clearing in the forest that was level and covered in a thick soft moss. It seemed almost like a mattress and was an ideal place to camp. We set up the tent just as the last light of the day left the sky, then we settled into our sleeping bags on top of the comfortable soft moss. Not every place we slept was so comfortable and it was a nice change to wiggle into the soft layer beneath us instead of the hard ground that we were used to.

I laid there thinking of all the warnings we had gotten up to that point on the trip, but everything had gone to plan so far. We had even got into Alaska without a problem which I didn't really think was going to happen. I heard a twig snap, but then there was silence – it must have just been a bird or a squirrel. I thought of all the bears we had seen that day, it was frightening to know how close they were to us. But we hadn't been bothered by any wild animals yet on our trip, so I reassured myself that any fears I had were all in my mind. Then I put my head on my pillow and drifted off to sleep.

I woke up in the pitch-black night instantly wide awake and alert. I couldn't explain why, but something felt wrong. I sat up and listened to see if it was a noise that had startled me, but the moment I became aware of my surroundings, I realised that my bed mat was moving. For a second, I sat still and wondered how it could possibly be moving. I listened for any sound beyond the thin fabric wall and I quickly became aware of something breathing heavily and I realised that whatever was outside was heavy enough to move my whole bed mat when it walked. All of a sudden the tent began to shake violently, the zippers rattled and I just sat there frozen with fear. For just a second things were silent, then I could hear the heavy breathing again and snorting as well. What could it possibly be? I wondered as I thought of all the animals I had seen that day. I knew it had to be a grizzly. They were hungry and it was feeding time.

I could hear the moss being torn by each individual claw with every step that the creature took as it circled the tent. Then it grunted and shook the tent again. I remained still, scared for my life while my heart raced. The words from the lady at the visitor centre echoed through my head, "You're guaranteed to see lots of grizzly bears."

AHHHH! I screamed inside my head as my fear turned to anger. Why didn't we buy the damn bear spray? How could we have been so foolish? Less than twenty-four hours earlier I had held the bottle in my hand. Erica had even told us that the bad berry season had led to hungry and desperate bears. Yet we didn't take her advice. Instead we decided to camp in a wildlife reserve full of hungry bears. We certainly made some good decisions I thought.

I scoured my mind, trying to think of a possible solution to our predicament. I imagined that I was the bear and tried to think what it was thinking. I figured that it was hungry and that we smelled like food. Then I remembered that we still had our toothpaste in the tent! There were signs everywhere that said, 'Do not camp with toothpaste or cosmetics in your tent.' How could we be so stupid? We had stashed our food but forgotten about the cosmetics.

The tent shook again, more violently than before and then the creature kept circling us. I was freaking out. I thought of all my possible options to stay alive. There was running away or climbing a tree, but the bear was faster and a better climber. Our only hope was to fight it, but that didn't seem like a great idea. I looked over at Heidi and somehow – God knows how – she was still fast asleep.

So the bear is hungry and it wants the toothpaste. What if I just throw it out of the tent? I thought. But I didn't want to meet the bear face to face. It seemed that the only thing keeping us alive was the fact that the bear didn't actually know what was inside the tent. It might think that it was a trap or dangerous. The bear started shaking and pushing the tent further than before, nearly hitting my face. My thoughts vanished. I looked over at Heidi, her silhouette barely visible in the darkness. I decided it was time to wake her up. I shook her leg gently, hoping not to startle her.

"WHAT?" she said, wondering why I was shaking her in the middle of the night.

"I think there's a bear out there," I said before the tent shook again. "Pass me your knife."

Heidi pulled out her tiny Swiss Army Knife with the one-inch blade. I opened it up. But then I remembered the size of the grizzlies claws I had seen on display in the tourist centre. The knife seemed useless in comparison.

But we had no other options. I remembered that grizzlies generally killed their prey and then buried it to let it rot for a few days before they ate it, assuming they weren't starving or desperate. I figured that maybe if we got mauled and just played dead, perhaps we could make it to the hospital before we bled to death. Thank God for the Canadian health care system, I thought, right before I remembered I was in the US with no travel insurance and no credit card. Wow, we did not plan our trip very well, I thought. We were in a great deal of danger and there didn't seem to be any shining light at the end of the tunnel. Even if we got mauled and survived, no emergency room in the USA would accept us without money.

"What do you think we should do?" I asked Heidi.

"I don't know, are you sure it's a bear?"

"Positive – and it can run, climb, and swim faster than us. I think it found us because of the toothpaste, I thought of throwing it out the door but I don't want to see that thing face to face."

"Neither do I," Heidi replied.

From the moment that we began talking, I noticed that the bears activity had slowed down. Then it sounded as if it sat down right beside the tent before letting out a big sigh. It seemed as if the last thing that we would be leaving for the world would be the form that we had filled out at the homeless shelter.

We waited in silence, listening to see what the bear did next, but it didn't move. I had already accepted that these may be the last few moments of my life. In my head I sent love to all my family, my friends, and to the bear. I was content with who I was and what I had done with my life. Even though I didn't always make the best decisions, I tried to learn from every mistake that I made. Each day I lived, I tried to be a better person than the one I was the day before. I put it out to the universe that I didn't want to die yet, but accepted that if it was my time to go I was ready.

I knew that the bear could probably smell my fear and thought that I was only making the situation worse by panicking. I decided to calm myself down so I took long deep breaths until my heart rate slowed and I was at last able to clear my mind. I could still hear the bears breathing deeply right beside me. I laid back down and waited for the bear's next move, but it never came and after a while I must have fallen asleep.

I woke up as the first rays of sunlight brightened the tent and was happy to see another day. I slowly unzipped the tent flap just enough to stick my head out and cautiously looked around. There was nothing to see but the forest. "Let's get out of here," I said to Heidi. Within a few minutes our bags were packed and we were rolling up the tent as quickly as we possibly could. When we were done, we ran out of the woods. Then we went and grabbed our food that we had stashed in a drainage tunnel and started our walk back towards the tourist centre.

I was happy to be alive and all I wanted to do was get out of Alaska as quickly as possible. Our fun adventure had turned into a nightmare and we had a long road ahead of us to get back to the border, let alone out of bear country.

We waited all day on the side of the road, desperate for a ride to take us anywhere. There were no buildings nearby and every time I heard a branch snap in the bushes I feared that we were being stalked by a wild animal. All we knew was that we didn't want to spend another night in Denali National Park. The hours in the day passed by slowly while we waited and hoped, but only a few cars went by. The odds seemed to be against us.

My optimism faded with the setting sun and I wondered if we would survive another night. Had we just got lucky the night before? We knew that no matter where we camped the bears would find us, they were everywhere. On top of that I had just found out that bears can smell food from thirty kilometres away. The day before we had seen more than ten bears in twenty kilometres. Things were not looking good.

Just then a truck pulled over and we gladly jumped in hoping to get away before we even checked where it was going. There was only one direction the highway went, so it really didn't matter. Once we were moving, we found out that the driver was only going ten minutes up the road into the middle of nowhere. The guy dropped us off in front of a decrepit old motel that still had the odd light on, but there were no cars in the parking lot and the place looked like a scene out of a horror movie. I dropped my bags and sat on the ground in despair, wishing that I was back in Whistler – the place I should have never left.

If I was going to die in Alaska, I was sure that the time had arrived. We were sitting on the road with our bag of food beside us and nowhere to go. The bears would have already picked up our sent and were quite likely walking towards us at that very moment. I looked at the run down building, but I didn't want to knock on the door. So we stayed where we were as the last rays left the sky and we hoped that another ride would come.

NEVER GIVE UP
Wasilla, Alaska. 10,539 km.

"A good laugh overcomes more difficulties and dissipates more dark clouds than any other one thing."
—Laura Ingalls Wilder

We were engulfed by darkness. We tried to come to terms with how another night would play out in the wilderness, but it didn't look good. Instead of going to set up camp, we just stayed on the road, waiting and hoping that a ride would come.

Then our prayers were answered when a black SUV pulled over, "Where you guys headed?" the guy behind the wheel asked.

"Anywhere but here!" I replied.

"Hop in, I'm Ben," he said with a smile. He was going to the next town, a place called Wasilla about eighty km south. We were saved.

"Where ya'll from?"

"Canada," I said.

"Oh, did you hear the story about how they named Canada?"

"No," I replied.

He chuckled and then said, "Well, back when they were trying to figure out the name for the place, a group of government officials sat in a room and discussed what to call the new country. They weren't having much success so the head official said, 'all right everybody, say a letter and I will write them down.' So the first guy said 'c, eh.' The second guys said 'n, eh.' Then the third guy said 'd, eh.' After writing down the letters he looked up at the room full of people and said, 'Okay, so how does Canada sound?' Eh." I thought it was hilarious. I had never heard that one before and it felt as if my laughter had taken a heavy weight off my shoulders.

Over the next few hours the jokes didn't stop and we were finally able to take our minds off the ordeal we had been through the night before. I noticed that as we got further south, the sky became lighter. I realised that it was because the mountain range that surrounded Denali National Park blocked the sun once it dipped below their peaks.

We pulled into the town of Wasilla in the darkness and the sight of houses and stores was welcoming. I felt a world away from where we had been only a few hours earlier. We hadn't had a shower for a while, so when we saw a laundromat that advertised 'hot showers' we went inside. But it cost five dollars for a minute, which seemed expensive and was out of our price range, so we left as dirty as we had arrived.

We searched for a place to camp for the night and eventually found a forest just beyond a chain-link fence within a residential neighbourhood. It seemed like an ideal spot to camp. Surely there were no bears near people's houses? There was a building that we could see on the other side of the forest that looked like a school, but we were happy to be in the middle of town instead of on the outskirts where the bears roamed.

We climbed over the fence and walked into the forest where we found a flat spot to camp. We set up our tent and went straight to bed. The air was a bit warmer than it had been further north and I was a lot more confident that we were not going to get eaten alive that night.

In the morning we woke up to the sound of children playing nearby and realised that we were in fact on school property. But none of the kids ventured near the forest and nobody bothered us, so we slept in.

We wanted to leave Alaska as quickly as we could, ideally before a bear mauled us. But when we looked at the map for a way back to Canada, we noticed we were within a hundred km of the city of Anchorage and it was too tempting to skip. Surely it was a built-up city with no bears? We decided to spend one last night in Alaska before we made our way home.

SHOULD WE STAY OR SHOULD WE GO?

Anchorage, Alaska. 10,609 km.

"You don't know, if you don't go."

I had hoped to get closer to nature by hitchhiking, but when the bear was shaking the tent I realised that I was happy to return to my normal life. I had been trying to escape society and all that comes with it – the busy roads, commuting, tall buildings, endless amounts of people – but as I stood there on the side of the busy highway with buildings all around I realised for the first time that I was happy to be engulfed by it all.

A guy named Eric pulled over in an old pick-up truck, he was headed to Anchorage to collect his dad from the airport but was already running late so we drove straight there. Then Eric took us downtown with his dad.

"Ya'll know that Anchorage has the second fastest tides in the world?" he asked us.

"Hmm, no I didn't know that," I replied.

"Yeah, it's a sight to see, but don't go wandering out into the ocean when the tide's out. Tourist's go out to get a pic, then get stuck in the mud right before the tide comes racing in. It's not pretty. Be careful out there ya hear?"

They dropped us off right in downtown Anchorage. The city was bigger than I had expected, full of tall buildings, restaurants, bars, and everything in between. Fighter jets blasted through the sky all day long. At first it was exciting to see them but after a while the whole city just felt like an airport runway.

The restaurants were tempting and the thought of eating a nice meal to celebrate being alive seemed like a great idea. But it was not a wise financial choice with the little money that I had left, so I decided to save my cash. We walked to the ocean and I stared at the big muddy plain. I wanted to wander out as far as I could, but remembered what Eric had told us. We sat on the bench and an ginger cat came to hang out with us. It was nice to have an animal to play with, especially one that I wasn't scared of.

The sun had set so we walked through the dark streets of Anchorage, looking for something to do. We found a bar with live music and we spent the next few hours nursing a drink and listening to the blues with all our bags beside us.

After a few hours, we walked the empty streets looking for a place to camp. There was nowhere good in the city, so we ventured away from the buildings until we found a property surrounded by trees to set up camp. Again I was relieved to be close to buildings, sure that there were no bears to be found anywhere nearby.

In the morning a stranger's voice woke us up.

"Good morning," a strange voice said, "sorry to bother you, but you're on US government property and you're going to have to get up and move."

I stuck my head out the door and said, "Good morning."

"I'm sorry guys, but you've got to go now, not everybody that works here is as relaxed as I am."

"Give us two minutes," I replied.

We threw on our clothes and packed up the tent as quickly as we could while making small talk with the security guard. He had gone about getting us off the property in the most pleasant way possible. I kept having flashbacks to the bear, the sounds of the claws tearing the moss, the heavy breathing. It was a constant reminder of how vulnerable we really were on the road.

It was a good time to leave Alaska. We looked at the map to see which road we should take to get back to Canada. But then we saw a little town just south of us called Homer a couple hundred km away. It didn't look that far and we were torn between wanting to see more of Alaska and trying to get home alive. So we decided that Homer would be our very last stop before we left.

We had to walk to the other side of the city to get to the highway, our bags were heavy and my guitar case felt like it was going to tear my arm off. We were halfway to the highway when we walked by a gas station. A lady pulling out of the parking lot, rolled down her window, and asked, "Where you headed?"

"Just down to the highway," Heidi replied.

"Well, I can take you there if you like."

Our dreams had come true. The walk had been long and painful and it was a relief when I finally put my bag down. I realised that every person we had met in Alaska had been extremely nice and we hadn't waited very long for most of our rides since we had arrived. Surely we would make it back to the border quickly and safely with the luck we were having with rides.

We jumped into the woman's small red Toyota and once inside, she said, "You guys looked a bit tired and I wanted to make your day a little easier." We thanked her for her kindness and before we knew it we were on the side of the highway. Why we were still exploring Alaska instead of going straight for the border, I cannot tell you.

THE THREE-LEGGED MULE
Homer, Alaska. 10,967 km.

"Sometimes in life you have to believe that things happen for a reason."

A rock embankment stood behind us on the edge of the highway and we were trapped between the cars spewing out exhaust fumes and a wall blocking any fresh air from blowing through to us. It wasn't an ideal place to stand, but there was no better place in sight. As each car went by, I tried to guess where the people were going, but of course there was never any way to know.

A blue four by four pulled over, a young guy named Josh was behind the wheel and driving straight to Homer. The scenery was greener than it had been further north, we drove past a big empty plain that I knew would fill up with water again when the tide came up.

"There's a great band playing in town tonight," Josh said. "They're called the The Three-Legged Mule. You have got to go, they're amazing!"

"Sounds like a good plan to me."

Josh worked up north as a contractor during the week then drove back home for the weekends. When we pulled into town, he took us out for a beer to show us the bar where the band was going to play that night.

We walked into the old pub, which was dark and smelled of stale beer. My eyes took a few minutes to adjust to the dim light and only then could I see that there was only one other person inside the place, a lone man sitting on a bar stool drinking a beer. Josh bought us a drink and after we agreed to meet him later that night.

We could only find one shop in town and all it had was overpriced groceries and cheap beer, so we left empty-handed. We wandered around looking for a place to set up camp somewhere close to the bar. Eventually we found a path behind some houses and we followed it until we found a flat spot to camp surrounded by bushes. We set up our tent, ate some peanut butter sandwiches for dinner, then hung out until the sun went down. Once it was dark, we grabbed our bags and walked back to the bar.

We found some bushes beside the venue and when we were sure that no one was watching we stashed our bags in them. We walked through the front door to a packed house full of merry drunk people. A few guys that were sitting at the table next to the door looked at us like we were aliens on the wrong planet. But another guy from the same table quickly said in a thick American accent, "Where ya'll from? I'm Pete."

"We're from Canada, we just hitchhiked up from B.C.," I replied.

"No shit!" he said, with an impressed look on his face, "Well, you better take a seat. Ya'll wanna beer?"

"Sure, thanks," we said as we joined his table and fresh beers were placed in front of us.

Everybody at the table was a pilot that flew small planes into the bush. They also did private charters, ferrying people in and out of fly-fishing and hunting camps, and they brought supplies to people who lived in the wilderness. But when they weren't working, they all lived in Homer.

A band started playing and the night was in full swing.

"Is that The Three-Legged Mule?" I asked.

"Shit no, that's just the first band," someone replied. "They'll be up later on."

Beers were only two dollars, so on my budget I knew I could afford a couple of them.

"Would you like another beer?" I asked Pete, hoping to take my turn buying a round, but he looked at me and said, "Let me get them man, the beers are on us tonight." With that he was off to the bar for another round.

A few hours and countless beers and shots later The Three-Legged Mule was well into their set of barn-stomping bluegrass music. The dance floor was packed with happy dancers stomping the night away. In fact, the whole bar had a great vibe and was full of nice people. Everywhere I went someone said hello.

It was well past midnight when the band stopped playing and it looked like the fun was about to wind down.

"Hey Pete, what time does the bar close?" I asked.

"Close?" he chuckled and then said, "when the party stops."

"But the band just finished, won't people start to leave?"

He laughed again and said, "Finished? Nah, they're just taking a break – they'll be back soon!"

I went up to the front to say hi to the band who were slowly making their way off stage. I started chatting away to one of the musicians when another one of the band members said, "Hey, why don't you come join us on our break?"

They led me out the side door of the bar and into a camper they had in the parking lot. Once inside they passed around some beers and a pipe. They told stories about the tour they had just done and I told them stories about my hitchhiking adventures.

After getting lost in conversation and beers, one of the band members said, "Shit, we should probably go and keep playing at some point, it's been a while!" Everybody laughed, then we made our way out of the camper and back into the bar. The band went on stage, the crowd erupted in cheers, and the dance floor filled up again.

The night progressed into the early morning and people slowly trickled out of the bar until the dance floor was almost empty. Heidi and I decided to go, and on the way out we said goodbye to all our new friends and thanked them for their hospitality.

"Do you guys need a flight somewhere?" the pilots all offered. "We can take you anywhere we're going."

They listed off their flight routes for the next week, but they all seemed to be going further into the bush. Although the offer of another adventure was tempting, both Heidi and I had our eyes set on the road home. I had been on the road living out of my backpack since I had left Whistler four months earlier and I looked forward to having some sort of stability in my life.

I was happy we had taken the trip to Homer, the great people we met made me forget about bears and I was finally able to relax again. We grabbed our bags and stumbled across the street to go down the path to our tent. But it turned out that finding path in the dark while drunk was a lot harder than it had been during the day. We walked in circles for a while, but eventually found the way to our camp.

When we woke up in the morning, we hitchhiked to a place called the spit that we had heard about the night before. The spit was a road that went seven km straight out into the middle of the ocean. Apparently at the end of the road there was a bar that had its walls inside covered in dollar bills, each signed by their owners before they left them. The tradition was to write your name on a dollar bill and place it on the wall. When we got to the end of the road there were a few fishing huts and buildings surrounded by docks and boats. One of the buildings was the bar so we went inside.

We got a couple of beers and then signed two one-dollar bills and stuck them up on the wall with the others. We had achieved our goal for the day and foolishly had a few dollars less than when we woke up. It was a waste of money considering the amount we had left, but we couldn't leave town without leaving our names on the wall.

Heidi went to the washroom, so I went outside and began hitchhiking to try to get us a ride. The first truck pulling out of the parking lot stopped in front of me and the driver said, "Hop in."

"Oh, actually I'm with my friend, she's just on her way out."

The driver looked in the back then said "Oh, sorry man – we've only got one free seat. Well actually we could arrange a few things, we don't mind."

I didn't want to be a bother, so I said, "Don't worry we'll grab the next ride, thanks anyways." He smiled and said, "Good luck," before driving off.

A few minutes later Heidi came out of the bar just as it started to rain. About twenty minutes later we were soaked. It dawned upon me that we were standing at the very end of the road, there was no place for traffic to come from other than the parking lot, so cars were going to be few and far between. I should have taken the ride while it was available, I thought. The rain got heavier and I started to worry that the water would seep into my guitar case. Everything else we owned was still sitting in the tent. I couldn't help but think of the ride I turned away as we stood there getting drenched.

A green Subaru wagon pulled over and the driver said, "Hop in, it's wet out there!" Without a moment's hesitation we jumped in. The guy's name was Jim and the back of his car was full of buckets, nets, hooks, boots, and random fishing gear.

"I've got a boat at the dock," Jim said, "I'm getting reading for our next fishing trip."

We chatted the whole drive back down the spit and when we were nearly on the mainland, Jim said, "Where are you guys staying tonight?"

"Just in the bushes in town," I replied.

"Well, I just had a wedding at my house last week and I have a little guest house. It's all set up and ready to go if you would like a dry place to stay for a night or two. There's power, a washroom, and it's private."

I looked at Heidi and then looked back at Jim. "We appreciate the offer, but our tent is already all set up, so we should be all right."

He said, "Well, the offer's open, it's no hassle to me. The place is just sitting there empty so if you change your mind let me know."

We kept chatting about other stuff until Jim arrived at the bushes near where we were camped. Just as we were about to get out Jim made the offer one final time. "Are you sure you don't want a place to stay? You don't even have to talk to me if you don't want to. I have another house on the same land, I just thought it would be a waste if I have an empty place and you need somewhere to crash. It's only a few blocks from here and if you don't like it you don't have to stay."

I could tell Jim was just a genuinely nice guy, but I didn't want to burden him.

"Our tent is already set up and it would take us a while to take it down. We don't want to waste your time."

"That's all right," he said, "I don't have anything to do today, I don't mind waiting if you want to pack up your stuff."

"All right, we'll be as fast as we can."

He smiled and said, "No rush."

We walked as fast as we could to the tent not wanting to

keep Jim waiting. When we arrived at it, we saw that our tarp had blown off the top and that the tent was full of water. Everything we owned was soaking wet. We drained the water out of the canvass then dragged it full of our stuff back to the car. If we hadn't accepted Jim's generous offer, it would have been the worst night of our trip. Well, apart from the bear incident.

We drove off with Jim and a few blocks later we pulled into the driveway of a cute two-story house. There was a boat in the driveway, a stage set up on the lawn, and a little cabin to the right of the house. Jim showed us the cabin and said, "Make yourselves at home, you're welcome to stay for two nights but you'll have to be on your way after that because I'm going fishing." The cabin had a large room with a nice big bed and a washroom.

"Thanks so much for having us, our night would have been cold and wet if we'd camped!"

"Don't worry about it, the house would have just sat here empty anyways. I will be hanging out in my place tonight, feel free to knock on the back door if you want to come and say hi later."

Jim left and went into his house. Heidi and I unpacked our bags and hung up all our soaking wet stuff in the nice warm room before we had a nap on the comfy bed.

When we woke up a few hours later it was already dark outside. I put on the driest set of clothes I could find and knocked on Jim's back door. I heard footsteps, then Jim opened the door and said, "Matt, come in. Have a seat – would you like a beer?"

"Sure, if you're having one," I replied.

It was a cosy little house that had wooden walls covered in pictures of family and big fish. Jim grabbed two tall cans of Sapporo out of the fridge and passed one to me. I cracked it and we clanked cans before we drank. I sat down on the comfy leather couch while he sat in one of the recliners before saying, "Tell me about your trip, you must have had a few wild adventures!"

The conversation flowed and while we were chatting, he pulled out a beautiful classical guitar and started tuning it. All at once everything made sense. He played a few songs for me and then passed it over and I played a few for him. Then I grabbed my guitar from the cabin and the fun began. I realised that he most likely picked us up in the first place because I had my guitar with me.

Heidi joined us and after a little more jamming, Jim looked up and said, "Hey, do you guys like candied salmon?" I laughed and told him about the jar we had been given earlier on the trip and how I gave it away to the guy with flames on the side of his truck.

He couldn't believe that we gave away a precious jar of candied salmon, then insisted that we try it ourselves. He pulled out a jar from the cupboard and placed it on the black granite counter. It looked as unappetizing as first jar did, but I knew there was no way for me to get out of trying it. Jim drained the juice out of the container and dumped the fish onto a plate, then said, "Help yourself." I grabbed a piece and put it to my tongue like a child trying something suspicious for the first time. I was surprised that it didn't have a strong fishy taste, instead it was deliciously sweet and melted in my mouth. The flavours seemed to penetrate every taste bud and I looked back at the plate for more.

I wished that I had something to share with Jim just to be polite. Then I remembered the bag of sweet chilli Doritos that I had in the room and went and grabbed it. The sweet chill flavour seemed to complement the flavour of the candied salmon very well. Jim cracked open another jar and the feast continued. We ate until our stomachs were full and our hearts were content and then the three of us spent the rest of the evening playing guitar and talking.

"Well, I think I am going to head off to bed," Jim said eventually. "Do you guys want to have a hot tub before you go to sleep?"

"No, it's all good thanks, we're super content."

"Well at least come and check it out."

We walked into the back yard and Jim showed us a big round horse trough. He pulled the cover off the top and it was full of water. He had insulated the sides with spray insulation, stuck a thick steel pipe through the middle and that was it, a simple home-made hot tub.

"How do you heat up the water?" I asked.

"That's the fun part!"

He grabbed a twenty-litre propane tank, screwed on a flame thrower attachment, then lit it up. Whoosh. Jim stuck the flame thrower into the metal pipe that ran through the middle of the hot tub and we waited. Not long after, steam started to rise off the water. I was amazed at how simple his hot tub was. It was cheap to build and he didn't have a huge heating bill every month.

Jim went to bed while Heidi and I soaked our aching muscles in the hot water. It was nice to be clean again. I remembered the last time had been in the hot springs, but it seemed like an eternity had passed since then, even though it had only been a week.

When we were leaving a day later, Jim and his fishing crew were in the yard baiting hundreds of hooks for their trip. We thanked him for everything, then walked down the driveway towards the highway to begin our long journey home.

I was happy that we had gone to Homer even though it was out of our way, the nice people there had made the trip worthwhile. It seemed like another world compared to most places that I had been to. It's a place that I would happily go back to visit any day if the road to get there wasn't so long.

THE LONG JOURNEY HOME
Glennallen, Alaska. 11,609 km.

"The only fears you have are the ones that you haven't yet conquered."

We looked at the two possible routes we could take to get back to Canada: the highway that we had already travelled or the road through the bottom of Alaska known as the Tok Highway. The Tok highway looked like it was a shorter distance, but it didn't appear that there was even a town along it. After a discussion we decided to take our chances on it, partly hoping to avoid Denali National Park again and partly hoping that it would get us home quicker.

I was tired. Tired of worrying. There was always something to stress about. Be it bears, our safety, getting home, or money. I was starting to just not care anymore. I reminded myself of the hitchhikers that I had met in Winnipeg when I first started my life on the road, they had no energy, no ambition, and just didn't care. They had lost their desire for more and I was starting to feel the same way.

I was over hitchhiking. I thought of how nice it would be to just take a bus all the way home, only I didn't have the money. I remembered reading something once that said, 'In life, you are exactly where you have put yourself.' I thought about how true that statement was. I wondered where I wanted to be in the future – surely not on the road with nothing to my name.

We got a ride that took us the five-hour journey back to highway one. The highway that we hoped would take us all the way back to Canada. We waited for hours but not one car slowed down and as the sun dropped in the sky, I started to think about bears again.

At last an old rusty blue van pulled over with music blasting at full volume on blown speakers. The people up front yelled out the window, "GET IN!" We jumped in the back, happy to finally get a ride.

The van sped off and the lady up front turned around and yelled, "WHERE ARE YOU GOING?" There weren't many teeth left in her mouth and while she yelled, she passed a two-litre Coke bottle to the guy that was driving who took a big swig out of it.

It was at that moment that I realised that the people driving us were insane. They yelled and screamed gibberish at each other above the deafening volume of the music. It was not our ideal ride, but Heidi and I decided to try to cover a bit of distance while we could. Even though something inside me told me we should just get out.

"WHERE ARE YOU GOING?" I asked in response.

"WE'RE JUST DRIVING AROUND, WE CAN GO

ANYWHERE YOU LIKE!" I pulled out the map and showed the lady where we wanted to go and she assured us that she could take us there.

Not long after a sign came up on the road that said, 'Old Alaska Highway One.' Shit, I thought, was that where we wanted to go or did we want to continue going straight? I asked the lady up front but quickly realised that she was way too drunk to be any help. As we approached the turn off, she yelled "EXIT OR STRAIGHT?" I said, "Take the exit," unsure of where we were supposed to go. I watched with dismay as the main highway disappeared and was replaced by a single lane heavily wooded road.

Shit. I could tell straight away we were going the wrong way. I wondered why we even took the ride in the first place. After ten minutes of driving down the road without seeing another car, the guy pulled the van into a car park beside a river. There were about ten cars and trucks in the lot. We could see the river lined with fishermen only fifty feet away.

As soon as the van stopped, we grabbed our bags, jumped out, and ran away without saying a word. They wandered off to the river with their booze, stumbling and yelling the whole way, while every head within earshot turned to see what the racket was about. We could not have ended up in a worse spot, far away from the main highway down an uninhabited road next to a river full of salmon… right where bears fed. I knew we needed to get the hell out of there quickly.

The sun was low in the sky and I estimated that there was less than an hour of light left in the day. I looked at the cars in the parking lot and wondered if we would be able to get a ride from one of them. I looked down at the river and I saw an overweight guy with a white beard wearing a Speedo, carrying a snorkel, and shivering uncontrollably. He walked up to a pick-up truck in the parking lot, put his gear in the back, and grabbed a towel.

The night was approaching quickly and it looked like he might be our only chance to get a ride back to the highway. I walked up to him and made small talk, but he stared at me suspiciously so I got to the point.

"I'm going to be honest with you, we're hitchhiking and just got a ride with those two drunk people. They took us here to the middle of nowhere and we are afraid to stay the night because of bears. We don't have much to offer, but if you are going back to the highway and don't mind letting us sit in the back of your truck, we would greatly appreciate it."

He stared at me, pondering the situation.

"If you don't want to drive us, that's okay as well, no hard feeling either way." I knew that he had walked past the drunk people while they were yelling gibberish at the top of their lungs. It made our plea a little stronger and at least backed it up with some evidence.

He said, "All right, throw your bags in the back and hop in the front." Yes! I thought. Back to the main highway, at least a little further away from the bears. The guy's name was Gary and after we got in the front of his pick-up truck he drove off. He was still wearing his Speedos; his lips were blue and he was shivering almost uncontrollably. "Did you want my sweater to warm up?" I asked.

"Nah, the heat will be working in no time."

"Were you swimming in the river?"

He replied with his chattering blue lips, "Yup, I go swimming in the river to collect fishing tackle that gets stuck on the bottom."

"Do you ever see bears out there?"

"Oh yeah, almost every day. One time I was in the river swimming for some tackle and a grizzly started chasing me, I was dodging it left, right, and centre. That was a scary day!" That reinforced my hypothesis that he was slightly mad, but he was probably thinking the exact same thing about us.

"But it's what I like to do with my time. A few years ago I injured my back at work, got a big payout, and now I just enjoy every day to the fullest."

While he talked, I wondered if he was secretly Santa Claus. He did have the white beard and he was very jolly. Gary turned onto the main highway and then dropped us off. We thanked him profusely, sure that our chances of getting mauled or eaten had just dropped significantly.

Heidi and I assured each other that we would pick our rides more carefully for the rest of the trip home. We shouldn't have got in the van with the crazy people in the first place. My instinct had told me not to, but my desire to cover some distance had come out on top. It was a dangerous game to play and if we didn't start making better decisions, we might end up somewhere we don't want to be.

FRANK AND THE
HUNTING LODGE
Tok Highway. 11,732 km.

"If life was meant to be hard and miserable, it would feel great to struggle and to suffer."

The setting sun gave the valley a golden red hue, and as I stared off into the distance I could hear wolves howling. As the last rays of the sun left the sky, cool air descended on the valley. Then a van with a few middle-aged ladies pulled over just before darkness set in.

They were headed to Valdez, Alaska. A place with majestic mountains and glaciers, somewhere that I had always dreamed of visiting.

"We can take you all the way to Valdez if you like?" one of the ladies offered. But it just didn't seem like a good idea. We didn't have proper winter clothes, our money was getting desperately low, and it was getting noticeably colder each day. On top of that we just wanted to get home.

Instead, we got dropped off at the turnoff to Valdez. Besides a lonely gas station there was no other sign of humanity in any direction. There was a fireworks truck sitting in the back corner of the parking lot, so we decided to set up camp behind it.

But as we were setting up our tent, the door of the truck flew open and a voice said menacingly, "Who's out there?" I could make out the shape of a shotgun in his hand from the dim trailer light.

I said, "Just a couple of hitchhikers, sorry to disturb you. Is it all right with you if we camp here for the night? We'll be gone first thing in the morning."

His attitude changed quickly, "Oh sure, that's okay, but be careful – this is bear country. Have a good night." He shut the door and we were left in silence. I guess he lived in the fireworks truck.

We finished setting up our tent and then laid down for the night. I thought of how far we had travelled that day and how lucky we were to get away from those crazy drunk people and the river. If we covered that much distance every day, we would make it back down to Whistler within a week.

The next morning we started hitchhiking at first light with hopes of making it back to Canada by the end of the day. While waiting a convoy of over a hundred military vehicles pulled up at the gas station. They parked their trucks, armoured vehicles, and artillery trucks anywhere they could. I wondered if they were going to war or if they were just on a training exercise. A short while later the engines roared back to life and they all drove off.

An old station wagon pulled over, "We're just going to the Native reservation up the road but we can take you close to there if you like?"

"Yes, that would be amazing – thanks," we replied before getting in.

A while later they pulled up outside a building. "This is the last building before our turn, so it's probably the best place for you to hitch from."

I looked at the old building just beyond the empty parking lot and wondered what it was. Then after careful examination I saw a sign under the door that said, 'Hunting lodge.' It didn't bother me, we had the whole day ahead of us and I was sure that it wouldn't be long before we got a ride. The air had a cool chill to it so I put a few extra shirts on under my sweater to stay warm.

We stood and watched the sun rise and then begin to fall. Afternoon had arrived and not one car had gone by the whole morning. I was cold and bored. The more I looked at the hunting lodge the more I started to worry about where we had ended up.

A man walked out of the lodge towards us with a cup in his hand. It was the first movement we had seen all day.

"You guys looked a bit cold, so I made you some tea with a drop of sherry in it."

Then as quickly as he had arrived, he turned and disappeared back into the lodge.

When I took a sip of the drink, I realised that it must be half sherry and half tea. We happily drank it, the heat from the hot water and the liquor seemed to warm us almost instantly. We spent the rest of the day waiting on the side of the road for a car that never came. By nightfall only four cars had driven by the whole day, and none had wanted to give us a lift.

Night time was the scariest part of the day in Alaska and each time it arrived I dreaded it. It was when the wild animals roamed free and hunted for food. I walked inside the hunting lodge and up to the bar, and after some pleasantries I said, "It doesn't look like we're going to get a ride today, is it all right if we camp on your property tonight?"

The tall slender guy with a strong American accent responded, "Sure, thas all right, why don't you come in and tell us yer story first? The first beer is on the house."

"Sounds great, but we might go set up our tent first before it gets dark, then we will come in and say hi."

"All right, see ya in a bit," he said.

We set up our tent away from the building so that we couldn't be seen, hoping to not bother anybody. Then we walked back into the lodge. The place was dimly lit and stunk of booze. Two middle aged guys were sitting at the bar and looked like they hadn't moved all day.

Heidi and I walked over and sat on a couple of the stools. I put out my hand and said, "Hi, I'm Matt."

The bartender put out his hand and said, "Jeremy, where are you from?"

After a bit of small chat, Jeremy said, "So what would you like to drink?"

I sheepishly looked at him, "I'm happy with anything."

"Well, the choice is yours."

"Any beer that's on tap is perfect, thanks."

He put a fresh cold beer in front of me, and the taste brought back memories of a more stable life. I drank it and the second I finished Jeremy replaced it with a smile and a wink. More than a few beers and a couple of hours later the bar filled up. Most of the people lived on a Native reservation and a lot of them were already drunk. A few of them came over and asked, "Where you guys from?"

One of the guys who had a big moustache, a red bandana, and long black hair pulled up a stool beside us, then said, "Hey brother, you play the songs on your guitar and I'll sing."

He got Jeremy to turn off the music in the bar and we jammed for a few hours while the beers kept coming. The guy's name was Frank, but he looked more like Cheech straight out of the stoner movies.

"So where are you guys staying tonight?" Frank asked.

"We're just camping beside the lodge."

His eyes widened as he looked at me in disbelief. "Brother, you're crazy! Do you have bear spray?"

I said "No," and the whole bar went silent while everybody looked at us in disbelief.

"You don't have bear spray man?! Don't you know where you are? This is bear country brother, you're going to get eaten alive!" Everybody in the bar looked shocked and people started chatting trying to find us some bear spray. Finally, Jeremy pulled out a can from behind the bar and said, "You can have this for the night if you promise to bring it back in the morning."

I thanked him and promised that we would bring it back. The worried look on Frank's face didn't leave and he said, "Do you know how to use that? You're only going to get one chance brother, if you mess it up it's all over. Then you got a big pissed-off bear and no way to stop it." He explained how to use it. I felt a little safer with the bear spray sitting on the bar, aware that when we went to bed we were going to at least have a chance if a bear showed up.

Frank and I kept drinking and jamming and as the night started to wind down, he said, "Hey brother, I have an extra house that I don't use, you can stay there for the night if you want. It'll be safer than your tent. I'm going to the toilet so have a think, I'm leaving when I get back," then he walked off.

I leaned over the bar and said, "Hey Jeremy, do you know Frank well? He offered us a place to stay, I just wanted to make sure it's a good idea."

"Oh yeah, Franks a great guy, you can trust him. But you better be careful with some of his friends. If he has offered you a place, it would be a smart decision to take it as it's not safe outside at night round here."

"Thanks Jeremy."

Just as I finished talking to Jeremy, Frank got back from the washroom, "So did you guys think about the offer?"

"Yes and we accept, thanks so much," I replied, "but our tent is already set up."

"All good brother, I'll wait while you pack up." After thanking Jeremy, we walked out of the bar with Frank, leaving the bear spray on the bar.

"Hop in the truck brother, I'll drive to your tent so you have some light to pack up." He hopped in the driver's seat and fumbled around with some tapes for a while until he found one that he wanted. Then he stuck it in the deck, turned on the engine, and the lyrics, "You see you don't have to live like a refugee (Don't have to live like a refugee)" started blaring out of the speakers while we drove the short distance to our tent. I had just seen Tom Petty at the Pemberton festival and his music reminded me of the road.

After we packed up we drove down the highway and then turned onto a dirt road before we arrived at a little wooden house with no lights on. Frank jumped out of the truck and unlocked the door, turned the power on, and then said, "I'll be back in ten."

We dropped our bags on the floor, happy to have a place to sleep for the night. I trusted Jeremy's opinion and from the second I had met Frank he had seemed like a good guy. He walked back in the door with an armful of firewood, some cheese, and some crackers. He filled the fireplace with wood, lit a fire, and said, "The food is for you guys, make yourselves at home. I'll come say hi in the morning." Then he drove off in his truck down the dirt road to join his friends.

I had been scared out of my mind at the thought of sleeping outside the hunting lodge. Apparently I had a good reason for worrying. I thought of the look on everyone's faces when we told them that we didn't have bear spray. Somehow fate (or possibly my guitar) had taken care of us again.

Frank woke us up early the next morning with a sad look on his face.

"Brother, one of my family members died last night from kidney failure. It's been a rough night; you guys are going to have to go. We have to sort some things out today, but here is my email address – let me know how the rest of your journey goes." We thanked him for giving us a place to stay, packed our bags, and said goodbye.

That morning when we walked to the highway, we knew that if a car drove past us we somehow had to convince them to give us a ride. There was no way we could pass up a chance to get away from where we were. We were absolutely certain that there were bears all around us. We knew that there were very few cars that went down this highway and that our chances of getting a ride were slim.

I was thankful that Frank had offered us a place to stay for the night and sad that someone with such a big heart had to deal with a death in his family. Without Frank it was quite possible that we would have been disturbed by a bear again, but we may not have been as lucky as we were the first time. I felt almost helpless, being so close to Canada yet so far away. I wished that I could just call a taxi to take us the rest of the way. But without money, life is just that much harder. We didn't have the option to take a bus or catch a flight. We only had people's generosity to rely on.

SO CLOSE, YET SO FAR AWAY
Tok Highway, Alaska. 11,836 km.

"If your method isn't working, try another method."

By noon, only two cars had driven by. With each hour that passed the night got closer and time was not on our side. I found it strange that days we wanted to go quickly dragged on and the days that we wanted to go slow seemed to race by. Time seemed to play games with us.

Down the road there was a rickety old camper driving towards us a lot slower than the speed limit. We danced and did everything we could to get them to pull over. The camper slowed down and then stopped. There was an elderly couple in the front and they asked, "Where ya'll headed?"

"Back to Canada."

"Well, we can't take you across the border, but we will take you to the gas station near it."

I had a box of granola bars in my bag and I offered it to them. They gladly accepted it and thanked us for the gesture. It was all we had to give them but I would have offered so much more to take us away from that desolate road. A while later they dropped us off at a gas station somewhere close to the border.

Very few cars were going south but we knew that we had to get out of Alaska and away from the hungry bears. Standing on the side of the road wasn't working for us, so we thought of other ways to get a ride.

We decided to start asking people at the gas station if they were going to Canada. That way we could meet them face to face and give them a chance to judge us in person instead of from a distance on the side of the road. A gentleman with a cowboy hat and a big moustache walked out of the restaurant. When he got close to us, we said, "Hi, any chance you're heading to Canada?" His name was Randy and he replied, "Well, I've just come over the border on business, but I'm going back in about an hour or so."

"Any chance we can grab a ride when you head back?" I asked.

"Tell you what. You keep hitchhiking until I get back and if you're still on the road, I'll take you to Canada. How does that sound?"

"Amazing, thanks so much!"

We watched as he jumped into the cab of his big Dodge truck and drove deeper into Alaska. It was nice to be near the border, I already felt safer knowing that I was close enough to Canada to get a ride across to a hospital if I really had to.

We continued hitchhiking with no success right up until we saw Randy's truck coming back down the highway.

When I saw him slowing to a stop I could not have been happier. We were going to make it back to Canada alive.

We threw our bags in the back and hopped in the big back seat.

"Thanks for picking us up, we really appreciate it," I said.

"It's no big deal, I drive across the border regularly." But to us it was a big deal.

When he dropped us off in the little town of Beaver Creek on the other side of the border, I couldn't believe our trip had been a success. I felt as if we were already home even though we still had a long road ahead of us. We had successfully hitchhiked to Alaska and back to Canada. It was beyond my wildest dreams. I felt safer in Canada knowing that if something happened to us we would at least be covered by our health insurance. It was a comforting thought. But I reminded myself of the long empty road that we still had to travel before we arrived back in Whistler.

ALIVE AND BACK IN CANADA

Beaver Creek, Yukon. 12,012 km.

"Sometimes when you need someone in your life, they appear before your eyes."

We watched the sun set from the side of the road but I wasn't as scared as I had been knowing that I was now back in Canada. Behind us there was an outdoor hockey rink that was fully fenced in, and we decided that if we didn't get a ride we would camp in there. We had just about given up when a Jeep Cherokee went by, then slammed on the brakes and pulled over. When we looked in the window, it turned out to be Erica, the girl who had told us not to go to the Arctic Circle.

Her Jeep was packed to the roof with bags, furniture, and clothing. She got out and we hugged, both happy to see each other again.

"Where are you headed?" I asked.

"To see my dad in Whitehorse and then I'm moving back down to the lower states."

The car looked like it had been packed in a hurry. The front and back seats were covered in stuff and we helped her rearrange it so there was room for us and our bags. Once we were in and driving away, we got the full story.

"I had a rough week," she said the moment the truck was moving. "I talked to the guy who got me pregnant and he wasn't interested in having a child and I didn't want to raise a child without a father. So I had an abortion and I still haven't told anyone." She broke down in tears. It was as if the universe had sent us to her to be her shoulder to lean on in her time of need. "What's even worse is that my mom called me the day after I had the abortion and said that she had a dream that I killed her grandson. They would disown me if they knew that I'd done it.

"On top of that, the whole dynamic of the house I was living in had changed since my roommate had her kid. I had to leave, so I just packed up and left. I'm happy to see you guys again since I don't have another soul in my life to talk to about this."

I was glad she had found us again. We pulled into Whitehorse and I noticed we were driving past the fence that I had stashed my treats beside.

"Hey, is there any chance you could pull over? I stashed something in the bushes over there that I didn't want to take across the border."

I walked back to the fence post and sure enough found my treats. The treasure hunt had been a success.

"You're welcome to crash at my dad's place with me tonight, I can drop you off on the highway in the morning,"

Erica said. The next morning Heidi and I gave her big hugs and reassured her that everything in life happens for a reason and that in time things would be back to normal.

It was strange to think that one of our first rides in Alaska also turned out to be our first ride back in Canada. It's funny how we are able to run into familiar faces hundreds of kilometres from where we had last seen them. It was a testament to how small the world really is.

A QUICK JOURNEY HOME
Whitehorse, Yukon. 12,458 km.

"The more you experience, the more you are able to understand."

There were more cars heading south in Canada then there had been in Alaska, which was reassuring. We got a ride in a transport truck out of the Yukon and most of the way through B.C. Then a bush paramedic in his ambulance drove us as far as he was going. He even insisted that we call our moms on his satellite phone. The trip home went by quickly and each ride covered a great distance, which suited me.

Late in the afternoon one day after a few more days of rides we got dropped off at a gas station in a little town called Lillooet, only a two-hour drive from Whistler. We were waiting for a ride when a Subaru station wagon parked up beside us. The lady went in the shop and on her way out she looked at me and said, "Matt?"

"Yes?" I said with absolutely no idea who I was speaking too.

She realised that I didn't recognise her and said, "it's me – Cheryl, from the Pemberton festival? You were my boss and you let me go see Coldplay, remember?"

I said, "Oh Cheryl! Hi, how are you?"

"Good! What are you doing out here?" she asked.

"We just hitchhiked to Alaska and are trying to get back down to Whistler," I replied. I looked at her car, but it was packed to the roof and didn't look like she could fit another thing in there.

She said, "Oh, don't worry about all that stuff. I can fit you in, we might have to rearrange it but I'd be happy to give you a ride. I wouldn't have seen my favourite band if it wasn't for you!" It was a nice way to end the trip. Cheryl had clearly not forgotten that I had insisted on her going to see Coldplay. In turn, she insisted on taking us back to Whistler.

Two hours later Cheryl dropped Heidi and I off at the bus stop in town. I thanked her for the ride and when she drove off I lay down on the pavement, happier than ever before to be back in Whistler, the place I planned to call home.

I felt triumphant, as if we had just completed a long hard quest and could finally rest for the first time in months. My worries and fears were replaced by joy and contentment. I knew that the knowledge and experience I had gained on my journey would be with me forever, even though it would take me months or even years to reflect on it all. I was a different man from the one who had left and I had no plans to go anywhere in the near future. I just wanted to enjoy life like everybody else in Whistler.

But when the topic of finding a place to live for the upcoming winter arose, I wondered if I could live outside for it. How hard could it be? If I could survive the winter, I thought it would be the ultimate proof to myself of how little I actually needed to be happy. I knew I didn't need much in the summer, but the winter was a whole different story. Freezing to death would be a serious concern every night. But I figured that as long as I used my common sense, it might just work.

A WINTER OUTDOORS
Whistler, B.C. 14,849 km.

"Everything in life is relative to your experience."

I had heard of a secret cabin in the woods on a mountain near Whistler. Heidi and I decided to try to find it, and if it was empty we planned to move in for the winter. After following rumours of huts up and down the mountains Heidi and I finally found the right shack and it was tiny. There were two sections to it, the entrance and where the bed lay. The door to get inside was only two feet by three feet, and it was a struggle to climb in and out of. Once inside the door I stood in a three foot by three foot entrance that was just tall enough for my six-foot frame to stand comfortably within. There were hooks on the walls and a few empty milk crates for storage. Near the roof of the entrance there were a few windows that provided dim light. The second part of the cabin was just beyond the entrance and was the same size as the double bed, but the ceiling was only four feet high there. Tall enough to sit up, but I had to crawl to get back to the entrance. It was as basic as it gets. Just wooden walls and nothing more.

The shack was built at the edge of a cliff, propped up on an uneven slope fifty feet above the river rapids below. I knew that a fall would be fatal so each day I made sure to take every step carefully. There was no electricity, no wood stove, and no means of warmth. Just a wooden frame with thin plywood walls. Over the week we moved into the cabin, then we put a padlock on the door and called it our home for the winter. We made a rule to not bring any food to the shack to keep the bears away. We now knew that they are creatures of habit and if they find food once, they will always return in the hope of more.

A few weeks later, my friend Sebastian came and I helped him build his own tiny shack beside ours. He had heard of our adventures and had decided to come and join us for the winter. We all got jobs, ski gear, and lived a normal life like everybody else, except for the fact that at night we had to hike up the mountain to go to bed. We got some lockers in a local ski lodge where we kept our ski gear and food and also got access to their hot showers.

Each day got colder than the day before until winter arrived and snow started to fall. Our hike up the mountain turned into a trek through the snow. At night I used two sleeping bags and a fleece blanket to keep me warm initially. But late in the month of December the temperature dropped to minus thirty for three weeks. It was the coldest I had ever seen it in Whistler and even the river froze into a block of ice. Before bed I had to put on three T-shirts, three pairs of socks, a pair of long johns, sweat pants, two sweaters, a winter hat, and winter gloves. Then I got into my two sleeping bags with the blanket inside. On the really cold nights I even closed the top of my sleeping bag over my head, as it was the only way to avoid getting frostbite on my nose and ears. Those three weeks were a test of our persistence and determination and although at times it was bitterly cold and miserable, we didn't give up.

The weather eventually changed and the rest of the winter stayed above minus fifteen, which seemed relatively warm after the cold snap. That was something I would never have thought I'd say. I realised that everything in my life was relative to my experiences. Minus fifteen only seemed warm after experiencing minus thirty. A five-hour drive only seemed long until I had sat in the car for ten hours straight. Twenty dollars seemed like nothing until it was all I had. There are many lessons I learned along my journey and perhaps many that I missed. But in the end my outlook on life changed forever.

A NORMAL LIFE AGAIN
Whistler, B.C. 14,849 km.

"You are never too old to set a new goal or to dream a new dream."
—Les Brown

I had proven to myself how little I really needed to be happy in life. I discovered that it wasn't a lot, but there were some things that I knew I preferred to have but didn't necessarily need. I learned that life is all about perspective and that if you look at it the right way it will always seem like you have more than you need.

In April 2009 I moved into a house with my brother in Whistler. It had been nearly a year since I had lived inside and I appreciated everything just that little bit more. Just having water to drink whenever I wanted felt like a gift. Turning on the heater for warmth was fantastic and being able to have lights to see made my evenings just a little more enjoyable.

Hitchhiking showed me a different way to live than what

I had been trained to know. For me it was a way to learn and to grow. It showed me that there is no difference from the person living on the street to the person driving a nice new car. We all love and we all hurt.

I had spent many days of my life dreaming about going to many amazing places, but I had never taken the initiative to go. In a sense I was lucky that my friend Ryan suggested going hitchhiking that one night over drinks. Without him I suppose I might have never left. It was the easy way, in a sense, having someone to go with. But it was also the hard way. There were no guarantees. I took the opportunity that presented itself and I grew on my own from there. At times I was lost but content, alone but happy, afraid but determined. All just to see what was waiting around the next corner.

Thank you for joining me on my adventure and reading my first book. If you enjoyed it, please consider leaving an honest review at your favourite online store.

—Matt Fox

About the Author

Matt Fox was born near Toronto, Canada in 1983. After his hitchhiking adventures he moved to Australia where he spends his days writing and surfing.

Made in the USA
Las Vegas, NV
09 July 2021